THE AMAZING SPIDER-MAN 2

Peter Parker returns with an amazing new adventure featuring villains from the movie of the same name, plus a whole host of other foes to defeat ...

STAYING SAFE AND HAVING FUN

As with any gaming, check out a game's rating before you play it to make sure it's age-appropriate. If you're playing online with others, remember that they're not real-life friends. Here are some top tips:

1 Talk to your parents about what the rules are in your family, such as how long you can play games for, or what websites you can visit.

2 Don't download or install games or apps to any device, or fill out any forms on the Internet, without first checking with the person that the device belongs to.

3 Take regular breaks—putting your console or mobile device down every now and then is not only good for your eyes, it will also allow you to refresh and improve your play.

4 If you're playing games when you're on the move, be mindful of other people, and look where you're going.

5 Don't forget—games are meant to be fun! If things aren't going well in the game, just take a time out and come back to it later.

6 Don't respond to any online conversations that are mean or make you feel bad. Let your parents know right away.

7 Never agree to meet someone you met online in person, and never send photographs of yourself.

8 Don't feel pressured to spend money on games or apps. If a game tells you to spend money, speak to your parents.

9 When you're online, be nice to other people. Don't say or do anything that could hurt someone else's feelings or make them feel unhappy.

10 Never give out personal information such as your real name, phone number, password, or anything about your parents.

CONTENTS

GAME PROFILES

18

110

89

60

CONTENTS

FEATURES

44

38

86

96

FOR THOSE WHO WANT THEIR GAMING TO BE SUPER

60 FOLLOW BATMAN'S INCREDIBLE ARKHAM ADVENTURE

Following super hero adventures is fun. Whether it's in comics, books, on TV, or the big screen, there's nothing quite like the thrill of watching caped heroes righting wrongs in the world. But do you know what's more fun than that? Actually playing as the super heroes, of course!

You can play as Batman, becoming a virtual detective in the shadows of Gotham, suit up as Iron Man, and do battle through the medium of puzzle games, or team up with friends to take down Shredder as the Teenage Mutant Ninja Turtles. You can even create a super hero yourself . . . or maybe a villain.

With such a rich, diverse line-up of games, there's lots of fun to be had, if you know where to look. We have super hero gaming covered from every possible angle. There are expert tips to turn you into a gaming hero, definitive rundowns of the greatest characters and moments, stunning cosplays, cool secrets, hidden gems you might have missed, and a whole lot more besides.

THE 30 MOST HEROIC MOMENTS EVER

POPPING A MASSIVE TMNT: BATTLE MATCH COMBO

30 Put down the pizza when you play *TMNT: Battle Match*. The Turtles themselves might be known for their love of the famous Italian food, but you'll need every last bit of focus to land big combos in this game. Quickly tracing a line of matching symbols through a dizzying sea of color and icons isn't easy but it feels incredible when you pull it off. It's also rewarding to see your high score soar as a result, as the icons you matched disappear in a fizz of color and special effects. If you manage it, then sure, treat yourself to a slice of pizza.

UNLOCKING THE SECRETS OF MARVEL PINBALL

29 There are a huge number of *Marvel Pinball* tables to play through. From Iron Man to Moon Knight, they all have a wealth of secrets to discover that will keep fans glued to the table for hours. The Infinity Gauntlet table is one of the coolest. To beat Thanos, you have to unlock all the Infinity Gems. Each gem challenges your pinball skills in a fresh way—time might slow down, mini-games might appear, one gem even flips the entire table upside-down. And this is just one of the 21 tables you can play on!

TAKING FLIGHT IN MAN OF STEEL

28 Superman does most of his fighting on the ground in *Man of Steel*, pounding and brawling with Zod's army. Except when he punches his attackers so high and so far away, he can fly after them and grab them in the air. Awesome! But now what should you do? Fly through nearby obstacles like trees, cars, signs, and anything else in your way, giving Zod's minions the ride of their life. These bursts of action are so fast, you can almost feel the wind rippling through your cape.

SWINGING AROUND IN THE AMAZING SPIDER-MAN 2

27 When you think of Spider-Man, what do you see? You probably picture him swinging through the air, as the buildings of New York City whizz past. So, of course, that'll be the first thing you try in a game featuring the web-slinger, and *The Amazing Spider-Man 2* gets it so, so right. You can swing on web ropes, slingshot yourself into the air, and run along walls. String these moves together into one flowing motion and you'll look super cool.

RELIVING THE CIVIL WAR MOVIE

26 The *Civil War* story line shook the world of Marvel comics when it pitted Captain America and Iron Man against each other for the first time. It was also a box-office smash as the plot of *Captain America: Civil War*. So it's no surprise that it's made its way to games, too. From *Marvel Pinball* to *Marvel Future Fight* to *Marvel Contest of Champions*, you can relive the drama and fight for your preferred side. You can even rewrite history and use Captain America or Iron Man to fight for the rival faction . . .

LANDING THE BIGGEST ATTACK IN ULTIMATE MARVEL VS. CAPCOM 3

25 In a game full of eye-watering attacks that splash glorious color everywhere, the Crossover Combination has to be the most spectacular. By pressing both assist buttons at the same time, every character on your team jumps into the fray and performs their super attack together. If you have the right combination of characters—Iron Man, Storm, and Nova, for example—the effects are as beautiful to look at as they are damaging for your opponent.

TEAMING UP IN THOR: THE DARK WORLD

24 Thor is one of the most powerful characters in the Marvel universe but even he doesn't fight alone. Whether it's in the comics or the movies, Thor has back-up from the likes of Odin, Sif . . . and even other characters that he doesn't normally interact with, such as Doctor Strange. So, playing as Thor in *The Dark World* means you can summon warriors to fight alongside you. No other game lets you play the part of the commander of a super-powered army. Sit back, as your soldiers swarm all over any potential threats, before returning to your side to await orders.

Glide towards the waypoint.

GLIDING THROUGH GOTHAM CITY IN THE DARK KNIGHT RISES

22 Gliding through Gotham City on your cell phone? It shouldn't be possible to squeeze a city of that size onto such a small screen. And yet that's exactly what the developer of *The Dark Knight Rises* has managed. Gotham City is captured here in its rainy, bleak glory—the tight alleyways, the towering skyscrapers, the pervading sense of fear. Yet for all that, the best moment comes when Batman spreads his cape and you take flight for the first time. Gliding through Gotham City, past buildings and across rooftops, is a truly awesome feeling.

TAKING DOWN A ROAMING HERO IN DC UNIVERSE ONLINE

23 The big world of *DC Universe Online* is brimming with life, but not all of it is friendly. And every now and then, there are notorious DC villains (and heroes!) roaming the world, waiting to strike at you should you dare to stray too close. These impromptu battles are brilliant because other online players will pass by, see the fracas, and then join in to help. What starts as a simple one-versus-one battle ends up with ten or more super heroes battling to take a powerful villain down, in a spectacle few games can match.

SMASHING HEROES TO BITS IN MIX+SMASH

21 In *Mix+Smash: Marvel Super Hero Mashers*, you're playing as super hero toys rather than super heroes themselves. What happens when a toy is hit by something as powerful as The Hulk? It smashes to pieces, of course. Building your own super hero toy is fun but nothing compares to the glee that comes from smashing your opponent's super hero toy to bits. Don't feel too guilty though—they quickly rebuild themselves to carry on the fight.

DOMINATING MARVEL CONTEST OF CHAMPIONS

20 *Marvel Contest of Champions* uses a star system to ensure fights are fair. A one-star Spider-Man will be matched with a one-star Scarlet Witch, for example. And that's how every fight is at the start of *Contest of Champions* . . . but if you put the work in, you'll eventually unlock a more powerful character with a higher star rating. You can then bring those characters to fights against one-star opponents and completely overpower them with stronger attacks and faster speed. After the exhausting battles that have come before it, it's a relief to start winning with ease, and a lot of fun, too.

HITTING NEW HEIGHTS IN JOE DANGER

19 This bike-driving, back-flipping, gravity-defying super hero can hit heights others can only dream of. Although tricky at first, you'll soon get the hang of the skills needed to make Joe Danger soar through the skies. There's nothing quite like pulling off a crowd-pleasing backflip at heights that will make you punch the air with joy, especially when pulling this off over shark-infested tanks or outrunning secret agents.

SEEING THE JOKER GET THE DOODLE JUMP TREATMENT

18 Mean, menacing, and always up to no good, The Joker is someone to be feared. But in *Doodle Jump*, he doesn't quite inspire the same fear. The Joker has been transformed into a cartoon and even though he's kept his wild hair, wicked grin, and yellow teeth, he's almost adorable. Which is something we never thought we'd say about The Joker. But seeing Batman take on his nemesis in cartoon form is brilliant fun because it's so different and unique.

TRIGGERING EXPLOSIVE ACTION IN CAPTAIN AMERICA: THE WINTER SOLDIER

17 When you throw Captain America's shield in *The Winter Soldier*, stand well back from the carnage that follows. The shield ricochets from enemy to enemy, making "DONK" noises as it pinballs around, but that's just where the fun starts. *The Winter Soldier* is packed with objects that just need a bash from Captain America's shield as it flies around to trigger mayhem. Streetlights come crashing down, hydrants burst open, explosive barrels blow up, and everything collapses and folds around Captain America like a house of cards. It's impossible not to smile at the mayhem that the game creates.

SOLVING ALL THE RIDDLER TROPHIES IN BATMAN: ARKHAM CITY

16 This is one of the toughest tasks to accomplish in any super hero game. The Riddler has set up 400 Trophies all over Arkham, and in order to catch him, Batman has to collect every single one. From well-aimed freeze blasts that create ice islands in sewers, to line launcher gymnastics to reach secret areas, you need to learn Batman's gadgets inside-out to beat The Riddler. You need to be smart, you need to be determined, and you need to be patient to collect them all. When you do, the surprising reward is well worth it . . .

SUPERMAN VS. SUPERGIRL IN INJUSTICE 2

15 We were treated to some incredible match-ups in the original *Injustice*. Seeing Green Lantern go toe-to-toe with Sinestro or Batman squaring up to Bane thrilled fans. But it was the stranger match-ups that delighted too, such as The Flash vs. Solomon Grundy. *Injustice 2* features the most intriguing match-up to date, as Supergirl's inclusion means we get to see her face off against her cousin, Superman. It's the first time ever that the family feud has appeared in a video game and it's sure to be explosive.

WOBBLING ABOUT WITH OCTODAD

14 He's mastered disguise, managing to live among humans without anyone suspecting a thing (we're not quite sure how Octodad has disguised his fishy smell). But what Octodad hasn't mastered is everyday chores—well, they're tricky if you don't have hands. Imagine trying to open a door or eat a meal without fingers. That's what life is like for Octodad, who can use his suckers to climb up walls, but can't even hold a fork.

CREATING YOUR OWN GAME

13 Sony's *LittleBigPlanet* series allows you to create your own game. You can craft fighting games, platformers, or even come up with your own genre altogether. So when Marvel released its heroes and villains for use in *LittleBigPlanet*, it meant that for the first time ever, you could create your very own Marvel games. So if you've been dreaming of a karting game starring Hulk, Green Goblin, and Magneto, try making it! It's time to set your imagination free.

DEFEATING JUGGERNAUT IN MARVEL PUZZLE QUEST

12 *Marvel Puzzle Quest* begins with easy quests against faceless agents, giving you a gentle introduction that teaches you how to play. However, that comes to a sudden end when towering supervillain Juggernaut appears. This is the first battle against an opponent with a massive pool of health and it's an exhausting showdown, as you would imagine against someone of Juggernaut's size. Chip away at his health for long enough, while surviving his head-rush attacks, and you'll win. After that, you'll feel like you can take on the world.

WIPING A ROOM IN MARVEL HEROES 2016

11 When *Marvel Heroes* first launched, the super attacks weren't particularly . . . super. Realizing this, the developers added extra punch and power for the free *Marvel Heroes 2016* upgrade. Now, all the super attacks have been amped up to bombastic levels, and using your powers now is like triggering an earth-shattering fireworks display. From the eye-lasers of Cyclops to the ground-shaking attacks of Hulk, *Marvel Heroes 2016* puts the "super" into superpowers.

PLAYING AS ALFRED IN LEGO BATMAN 3

10 Have you ever wondered what it would be like to see Bruce Wayne's butler, Alfred, fighting on the frontlines? Wonder no more. In LEGO *Batman 3*, you can unlock Alfred as a playable character. He uses his trusty tea tray as a shield and throws it like a boomerang to take out distant threats. Best of all, even in combat, Alfred has the same dry wit that he serves up as Batman's mentor, ally, and friend. In fact, we might even prefer playing as him to being the caped crusader!

SPIDER-MAN FANS FINALLY GET THE GAME THEY DESERVE

9 Whether it's through the brilliant sci-fi weaponry powering the *Ratchet & Clank* series or the awe-inspiring exploration in *Song of the Deep*, Insomniac Games has blown the world away with its creative games. So, the announcement that Insomniac Games would be making a new *Spider-Man* adventure is news that will make any fan of the web-slinger weep with joy. Swinging through a beautifully recreated New York City and fighting off Spider-Man's toughest foes has never looked so good!

ENJOYING THE FIREWORKS IN MARVEL FUTURE FIGHT

8 *Marvel Future Fight* is a feast for your eyes. The special moves burst with life and color, as lightning, fire, and sparks fill the screen with mayhem. Better still, the creators of the game understand what fans want, so you can perform special moves over and over again. And switch to other squad members as soon as you run out of special moves. And call in extra help so that assisting characters can do their special moves, too. In fact, you get to pile on layers of chaos and anarchy through the endless special moves, and the result is stunning to look at (and unfortunate for any foe who gets in the way!)

CREATING A WEIRD TEAM IN LEGO DIMENSIONS

7 When you think of a crime-fighting team, you think of the Teenage Mutant Ninja Turtles, or The Avengers, or maybe even the Justice League. But what you don't think of is Homer Simpson teaming up with Harley Quinn and The Joker. Yet that mix-and-match appeal is why LEGO *Dimensions* is so much fun, especially as it has so many characters picked from fan favorites like *Ghostbusters* and *Jurassic World*. Create a team that makes no sense to anyone but yourself and then take on the world.

SOLVING A CRIME IN BATMAN: ARKHAM ORIGINS

6 We've seen Batman, the caped crusader who fights for justice. We've seen Batman, the Dark Knight who watches over the skies of Gotham. But rarely do we get to see Batman as a detective, giving his brain, rather than his muscles, a workout. *Arkham Origins* gives Batman a chance to show how smart he is. He enters crime scenes, scans for evidence, and starts piecing together what happened. Batman will even put together a reconstruction of events in his mind, allowing you to spot more clues and evidence, if you're smart.

BEATING SHREDDER IN MUTANTS IN MANHATTAN

5 The final battle in *TMNT: Mutants in Manhattan* pits the foursome against their old nemesis, Shredder. To add extra drama to the showdown, the battle takes place on a platform floating perilously above New York City! The floating platform also tilts and sways while the battle takes place, which makes it even harder to keep track of Shredder. The encounter squeezes every drop of skill out of you and demands strong teamwork, as Shredder slices and slashes at the Turtles with his razor-strapped fists.

UNLOCKING A NEW HERO

4 Whether it's *Marvel Future Fight*, *Mix+Smash*, *Uncanny X-Men*, or any of the other many super hero games available on mobile, one of the thrills common to them all is unlocking a new hero to play with. You often don't get to choose, which makes it more fun—you could end up with an old favorite like Iron Man or Spider-Man, or discover a brand new favorite, an unsung hero like Phil Coulson or Spider-Gwen. It's the same feeling you get when you open a really great present on your birthday, but even better—because this doesn't just happen once a year.

PUNCHING SOMEONE THROUGH THE EARTH WITH DOOMSDAY

3 *Injustice: Gods Among Us* proves that sometimes, playing as the bad guys is fun. Superman's nemesis Doomsday is one of the biggest and baddest there is. He can leap into the air before crashing down on you, he can shoulder charge from distance, and he hits like a truck. Doomday's Super Move sums up how powerful he is. Called "Merciless," he throws his foes to the ground then pummels them through the Earth. When they emerge on the other side of Earth, Doomsday pummels them all the way back!

HOVERING OVER METROPOLIS AND GOTHAM IN DC UNIVERSE ONLINE

2 This is how it feels to be a real super hero. Picking "aerial" when creating your character in *DC Universe Online* grants you the power of flight, so you can soar above the skies of Metropolis or Gotham. From there, you can watch above your home, picking out the details—clouds passing as day turns to night, cars passing by on the streets below. You might even see a fellow super hero flying past! There's a strange tranquillity to looking over the awesome sight that is Metropolis and Gotham, but it's not long before you have to swoop back down to street level to fight crime.

TAKING BACK ARKHAM ASYLUM

1 The Joker's brilliant plan was to let Batman capture him. Batman then duly delivered him to Arkham Asylum where, with the help of a corrupt guard, the Joker broke free from captivity and let the other inmates go. Realizing there's more to this than a simple asylum takeover, Batman decides to work out and stop whatever plan The Joker has. And so *Arkham Asylum* begins and nothing makes you feel like a super hero quite like this game does. You feel powerful, as you use Batman's wide array of moves to combat goons. You feel smart, as you creep around each room in the shadows, avoiding the watchful glares of the guards on patrol. You feel like a one-man army, when you call upon a dizzying array of gadgets from grapple hooks to Batman's X-ray-like "Detective Vision" to clear the path ahead. Best of all, you feel like Batman, as Alfred encourages and guides you through your earpiece and you face-off against the likes of Bane and Poison Ivy.

MEET THE SUPERFAN

Adrian was first inspired when watching the *Batman* TV series starring Adam West. His costume looks much more serious than that one, though!

ADRIAN LIGHTON

WHY?

"Why did I choose to cosplay as The Batman? Well, it stems from my childhood love of the character—who I used to draw almost on a daily basis—and from watching the old original Adam West *Batman* TV series," says Adrian. "Who wouldn't want to don the cape and cowl of a true super hero with no special powers and deal out justice the way only Batman can?"

HOW?

"The costume I wear is sourced from around the globe, including from Canada, America, and Ireland," Adrian explains. "It's been well worth the waiting and countless hours researching prop makers and costume designers."

WHAT MAKES THE ULTIMATE SUPER HERO?

IT TAKES MORE THAN AN EYE-CATCHING COSTUME AND A COOL NAME TO BE A SUPER HERO. WHAT EVERY SUPER HERO REALLY NEEDS IS ...

... A SHARP MIND

IRON MAN, MARVEL FUTURE FIGHT

Behind the glistening red and yellow metal of the Iron Man suit is the sharp mind of Tony Stark. As the genius who built the suit, Tony Stark's brain power is one of the most valuable assets the Avengers have. *Future Fight* shines a spotlight on that brain power, as Iron Man is one of the few Tech characters in the game. Future Fight also gives us the rare chance to play as Tony Stark's Hulkbuster creation, the enormous suit he built specifically to fight The Hulk.

... INCREDIBLE STRENGTH

THE HULK, ULTIMATE MARVEL VS. CAPCOM 3

You don't need bulging biceps to be a super hero, but it certainly helps! Most super heroes have super physiques and The Hulk is the biggest and strongest of them all. In *Ultimate Marvel vs. Capcom 3*, he's so strong, he can shrug off weaker attacks like they're mere insect bites. This makes Hulk virtually unstoppable.

...THE ABILITY TO FLY

SUPERMAN, MAN OF STEEL

If you could have any super power, what would you have? Most people would say the power of flight, and it definitely makes Superman's job easier. Not only does flying allow him to ignore borders (and avoid public transportation!) but more importantly, it gives him an edge in combat. He can glide around the sky to stay out of his adversary's grasp and strike back from above.

...A NEED FOR SPEED

THE FLASH, INJUSTICE: GODS AMONG US

How can you stop someone you can't see? That's what villains will ask themselves as The Flash runs circles around them. He gets to show off his super speed in *Injustice: Gods Among Us*. When he activates super speed, time slows down for everyone except him. The Flash can use this time distortion to land attacks before opponents even have a chance to block or even realize what's happening.

...AN ARRAY OF GADGETS

BATMAN, BATMAN: ARKHAM CITY

Whatever the situation, Batman has the perfect gadget for the job. Arkham City throws some crazy stuff at the Dark Knight but he's got it covered. Armed thugs? Batman's Disruptor will jam their guns. Guards blocking an entrance? Sonic Batarangs will distract them. A switch you can't see? A Remote Batarang will hit it. Water indoors that needs to be crossed? A Freeze Cluster will create a small ice island. *Arkham City* throws some crazy stuff at the Dark Knight, but he's got it covered.

... A DASTARDLY VILLAIN

SHREDDER, TMNT: MUTANTS IN MANHATTAN

What's a hero without a villain to defeat? Bored and unemployed. The best heroes are those with adversaries who are their equal— like Batman and The Joker, Superman and Lex Luthor, Wolverine and Sabertooth. Just imagine what *TMNT: Mutants in Manhattan* would be like if you didn't have the pay-off of a battle against Shredder at the end? After all, it's the strength of their metallic foe that forces them to work together as a tightly knit group!

... A SLICK VEHICLE

BARREL BLASTER, SKYLANDERS SUPERCHARGERS

Not all super heroes are blessed with flight like Superman or super speed like The Flash. When that happens, it's useful to have a vehicle to get around in. That vehicle will need to be practical but also something that inspires respect or fear, like Ghost Rider's flaming motorbike. Or it could just be something that looks cool, like Donkey Kong's Barrel Blaster in *Skylanders SuperChargers*, which uses barrels for wheels! When it comes barrelling toward you (sorry), you can't help but laugh at how ridiculously awesome it is.

... A HUGE WORLD

METROPOLIS, DC UNIVERSE ONLINE

Every hero needs an interesting world— somewhere to live, somewhere to prosper, and somewhere to fight for. Superman's sunny home of Metropolis in *DC Universe Online* is a great example, and it has famous locations you can visit like LexCorp, S.T.A.R. Labs, and Stryker's Island. You can even take a guided tour around Metropolis from Booster Gold.

WHAT MAKES THE ULTIMATE SUPER HERO?

JANE FOSTER, MARVEL FUTURE FIGHT

Whether it's Spider-Man longing for Mary Jane Watson or Wonder Woman's relationship with US Army Officer Steve Trevor, super heroes need love, too. What's even better is when those love interests turn out to be super heroes in their own right. After her romantic relationship with Thor, Jane Foster ends up wielding the hero's legendary hammer, Mjolnir, when he loses his powers. She becomes known as Thor in his place.

... A STRONG SIDEKICK

LOCKHEED, UNCANNY X-MEN

Sometimes having someone you can trust and rely on fighting by your side is the most valuable thing in the world, no matter how super you are. Take Kitty Pryde of the X-Men. Her phasing power is strong, but alien dragon Lockheed adds an extra element to her attacking powers. He can breathe fire and fly at distant enemies, eliminating them quickly and quietly.

... A WISE MENTOR

WONDER WOMAN, DC UNIVERSE ONLINE

All super heroes have to start somewhere and their journey often begins under the supervision of someone who is wiser and more experienced. Wonder Woman proves a great example of a mentor in *DC Universe Online*. Despite her own struggles against Circe, Wonder Woman finds time to teach you magic and she'll team you up with allies, like Doctor Fate. Best of all, after each mission, she'll give you plenty of useful equipment and gadgets.

STATS

70 years of Marvel history represented by costumes and characters

Over 55 playable characters

8 downloadable characters in *Marvel Ultimate Alliance*

10 friends can team up to take on bosses

Over 100 Marvel characters

WE CAN BE HEROES

MARVEL HEROES 2016

DID YOU KNOW?
Marvel Heroes has been awarded 'Most Improved MMO,' showing how much the game continues to improve after launch.

★ **This might be the fastest game you'll ever play.** *Marvel Heroes 2016* adds the heroes and villains you know and love to the MMO genre, before cranking the speed up to eye-popping levels. This isn't a slow, traditional MMORPG like *World of Warcraft*. This is an MMO fit for the modern age and comic book fans. You and your friends pick your favorite heroes and get stuck into missions, which range from battles against towering foes such as Sentinels, to a race against the clock to save civilians in peril. It isn't just about mindless speed either—it even has a full story mode. Between missions, you can also tinker with the gear you've collected to see what armor, weapons, and clothing will give you the best stats and make you even stronger. Best of all, the developers are constantly improving the game and adding new characters.

TIPS & TRICKS

★ **OPEN WITH YOUR BIGGEST ATTACK**
As there are so many enemies in each mission, you should open with your biggest attack when you find them.

★ **LEVEL UP IN STORY MODE**
The Story Mode in *Marvel Heroes 2016* is the most efficient way to level up, so make sure you give it a try and remember to do extra quests between the bosses!

★ **TRY COSMIC DIFFICULTY**
Cosmic is the name of the hardest difficulty and it's worth trying. The rewards you can earn for completing it are *much* better than in the other two difficulties.

TOP 5 PLACES TO HANG OUT

ASGARD

2 Home of Thor, Loki, and Odin, among others, Asgard is the easily the most stunning location in *Marvel Heroes*. It's not just because of the towering, golden architecture that dominates the view. It's because of the glittering beauty of the Bifrost Bridge. Just try not to ruin the bridge during any fights that take place there!

HELL'S KITCHEN

1 This is the area of New York City where Matt Murdock, aka Daredevil, was born and raised. Your main mission is to deal with the threat of super villain Shocker, who has taken over the streets of Hell's Kitchen. There are also random events you can take part in, other players you can trade with, and an abandoned subway full of trouble . . .

MADRIPOOR

5 This square map might be small but it packs plenty of punches. It's home to the "Snakes in the Grass" quest, which puts you up against the tricky Kullen Gar. You'll also find Gorgon lurking, an opponent so difficult even Wolverine admits to being scared by him. If you want to test your skills, this is where to come.

SAVAGE LANDS

4 Savage Lands is a prehistoric tropical land in Antartica and it is full of dinosaurs. Of course. In the comics, Savage Lands is home to *Uncanny X-Men* adventures and in *Marvel Heroes*, it's home to some of the harder quests. It's tough but the rewards are worth it. You might also run into Sauron, the dinosaur-like nemesis of the X-Men . . .

MANHATTAN

3 The biggest expanse in *Marvel Heroes* and where you'll be doing most of your quests, particularly as you level up your characters and make them stronger. Whether it's saving citizens, putting a stop to rampaging Sentinels, or reliving the events of the *Avengers* movie, there's always something to do in Manhattan.

★ **SWITCH CHARACTERS OFTEN**
When you hit level 25 with a certain character, you'll gain a permanent bonus across *all* your characters.

★ **TAKE YOUR TIME IN BASE**
When you get back to base, any boosts you're using are frozen, so they won't expire. That means you can take your time to check all the gear you picked up.

SUPER SKILLS

The eye-popping display of powers the Marvel heroes exhibit is enough to strike fear into the vilest of villains.

| BRAVERY |
| MISCHIEF |
| DESTRUCTION |
| TEAMWORK |
| FUN FACTOR |

STATS

1,500,000
YouTube views for launch trailer

15 chapters
in total

Over 200 playable characters

9 downloadable character packs

THE BIGGEST DC COMICS PARTY EVER

LEGO BATMAN 3: BEYOND GOTHAM

DID YOU KNOW?
Movie director Kevin Smith, who named his daughter Harley Quinn Smith after the Batman character, is playable in the game.

☆ It was no surprise to see a third LEGO *Batman* game after Brainiac had rumbled into view at the end of LEGO *Batman 2: DC Super Heroes.* But what is surprising is how much has been crammed into *Beyond Gotham.* Besides the puzzle-solving, platforming, and punching, you can play around with powers such as flight, electricity and magnetism. Characters are accompanied by their famous theme music—you'll never tire of listening to Superman's iconic tune—while the Lantern planet levels are great to look at. But the beating heart in the center of *Beyond Gotham* is its sense of humor. It puts heroes in awkward situations and pokes fun at their attempts to avoid looking stupid. Who wouldn't want to see Cyborg pretend to be a washing machine to fool a security camera?

TIPS & TRICKS

★ UNLOCK FIGHT CAPTIONS
Select "Extras" then "Enter Code" from the pause screen. Then type in EWTPKA to unlock fight captions, making the combat even funnier!

★ UNLOCK ALFRED (1966)
In the Batcave, go to the docks and enter the pipe on the right with Atom. Keep pushing forward and you'll see Alfred's unlock token on the left.

★ UNLOCK CATWOMAN
Smash up the giant chess board in the Batcave, then use the bricks to create a bishop and queen. When the king is in checkmate, you'll get Catwoman's unlock token.

TOP 5 DOWNLOADABLE PACKS

GREEN ARROW

Fans of *Arrow* will love this downloadable pack. It's stuffed full of characters from the TV show—including John Diggle, Felicity Smoak, and even Malcolm Merlyn. It also picks up just after a shipwreck, and focuses on a showdown between Oliver Queen and Deathstroke.

MAN OF STEEL

Mirroring the beginning of the movie, the *Man of Steel* downloadable pack sees you saving Superman from General Zod and his forces, who have invaded Krypton. It's a fun level to play through but the highlight is the new characters you get to play as, including Superman's dad Jor-El. Look out for the surprise cameo appearance from original Batman actor Adam West, too.

HEROINES AND VILLAINESSES

The *Heroines and Villainesses* pack has a staggering number of characters. It includes Raven, Power Girl, Starfire, Vixen, Mera, The Spoiler, Killer Frost, Plastique, Batwoman, and Terra. Best of all, you can use this free pack with the other existing characters to put together the famous Teen Titans squad from the comics as well.

THE SQUAD

Captain Boomerang, El Diablo, Katana and Deadshot all take time out from tormenting Batman to form The Squad. This new team of misfits and criminals have to smash their way through Belle Reve Penitentiary to track down an infiltrator who wants to dig up all of their secrets. Characters such as Deathstroke join during the mission, and there's a dance party just before the finale!

BIZARRO

In his battle against Darkseid, Bizarro has created his own super heroes . . . but it hasn't quite gone right. Bizarro's crew of Batzarro, Bizarra, GreenZarro, and Cyzarro are based on known superheroes but have something slightly odd about them. For example, Batzarro is Batman but with his cowl on backward, so he can't see where he's going.

SUPER SKILLS

He normally works alone but Batman shows the true power of teamwork in this hilarious DC Comics mash-up.

| BRAVERY |
| MISCHIEF |
| DESTRUCTION |
| TEAMWORK |
| FUN FACTOR |

★ **UNLOCK THE QUESTION**
In the Watchtower Lobby, go to the left platform and use your super senses. Use your magnetic power to open the blue crate and find The Question's unlock token.

★ **UNLOCK THE RIDDLER**
In the Hall of Justice, there's a quest where you have to pass three riddles. Do this and you'll earn The Riddler's unlock token.

ROBIN SCARED OF RATS

He might be Batman's sidekick but Robin doesn't have quite the same sense of courage. An early trek to the sewers sees Robin scrambling for safety at the mere sight of rats! "Bats and rats aren't that different," offers Batman, who seems to be exasperated by Robin's lack of bravery.

ALFRED'S LIGHT SNACK

While Batman and Robin are trying to piece together the clues on Joker's next move, Alfred checks in to see if the duo are hungry. He returns with what he calls "a light snack" . . . a mountain of food so tall that it wobbles precariously when Alfred wheels it into the Batcave.

LEGO BATMAN 3: FUNNIEST MOMENTS

"HAWKMAN" TRICKING SECURITY

Lex Luthor disguises himself as Hawkman to sneak into the Hall of Justice but he has to pass a security check from one of the cameras first. How does he convince the camera that he's actually Hawkman? By squawking and pretending to flap his wings, of course.

GRUNDY GETS STUCK

Grundy is the butt of several running jokes through LEGO Batman 3, such as his awful smell and inability to keep up with what's going on. But the funniest part is when the villains clamber out of a manhole to break into the Hall of Justice and the giant Grundy gets stuck.

THE FLASH DOING HIS CHORES

When the Justice League are summoned to action, we're treated to quick montages of all of the heroes in action. All of them except for Flash that is, who is in the middle of tidying up his apartment ... so he uses his super speed to finish up before darting off to join the others.

ELECTRIC BUZZER

When Lex Luthor tells The Joker off for playing around, The Joker throws him an electric buzzer. When Luthor catches it and it shocks him, The Joker then reels off the best line in the whole game: "Your hair is standing on end ... I guess it's just your eyebrows." That's why he's known as The Joker!

ROBIN'S SPEECH

Robin is convinced that he broke Brainiac's hold over Batman by giving a speech about friendship. This forms the best running joke in LEGO Batman 3, as Batman insists otherwise. The final punchline is when Batman gives up and uses a friendship speech to save Superman.

THE EXPERT SAYS...

ROSS HAMILTON
Games Writer

The LEGO game series isn't just fun because of the gameplay. Even when the source material is pretty serious, the games still manage to insert their own unique humor into any situation. Whether it's a character slipping on a banana skin and totally wiping out, or cutscenes that show The Flash doing his household chores in record time, these little jokes are what make the games unique.

Add in Batman's one-liners, his annoyance at Superman being all-powerful, and his love of the color black, and you've got some of the funniest running jokes in any game series. Plus, playing LEGO Batman 3 has gotten me even more excited about the upcoming LEGO Batman Movie!

RELIVE FAMOUS MOVIE MOMENTS

THOR: THE DARK WORLD
Thor: The Dark World

There are a few differences between the game and the movie of *Thor: The Dark World*. Thor has more help in the game, thanks to Einherjar and various allies backing him up in combat, and he has to take on firehounds, berserkers, and other hideous creatures that weren't present in the movie. But the storyline remains the same—Thor has to deal with his treacherous brother Loki and ultimately, put an end to villain Malekith's evil plans.

AVENGERS: AGE OF ULTRON
Marvel Heroes 2016

If the revamped tutorial to *Marvel Heroes 2016* seems familiar, that's because it now apes the Avenger's battle against Ultron. While Ultron's sentries have taken over New York City rather than Sokovia, as in the movie, it's still reminiscent of the dramatic battle in *Age of Ultron*. You play as Captain America, Thor, Hawkeye, Black Widow, and The Hulk, beating down Ultron sentries while learning the basics of the game.

BATMAN V SUPERMAN: DAWN OF JUSTICE
Injustice: Gods Among Us

If you want to experience the battle between Metropolis' and Gotham's finest for yourself, what better game to play than *Injustice: Gods Among Us*? The storyline in *Injustice* sees the two super heroes at odds with each other, although the plot is completely different to *Dawn of Justice*. But, crucially, you can decide who you play as in the Batman vs. Superman showdown. Are you Team Bat or Team Man Of Steel? As a bonus, you can also experience the epic and exhausting battle between Bane and Batman from *The Dark Knight Rises*.

MAN OF STEEL
Man of Steel

If you were moved by the drama and action of the final battles in *Man of Steel* on the big screen, then you'll love taking part in them on the little screen, too. The last few levels of *Man of Steel* see you taking on Zod's lieutenants in combat before your final showdown with Zod himself. Just like in the movie, this battle shifts all over Metropolis as the two Kryptonians battle among construction work, fly through buildings, and fight in mid-air.

GREEN LANTERN
Injustice: Gods Among Us

Although the Sinestro of the *Green Lantern* movie hasn't yet become the infamous Yellow Lantern who trades on fear, he still has a great fight scene with Hal Jordan as part of the rookie's training. You can replicate their fight in *Injustice: Gods Among Us* and Hal Jordan even has the mini-gun light construct that he uses in the movie against Sinestro.

FANTASTIC FOUR
Marvel Ultimate Alliance

Whether it's the bright and breezy 2005 movie or the grittier 2015 reboot, Fantastic Four versus Doctor Doom is one of the classic Marvel battles that will be fought again and again. Fortunately, you get the chance to relive this encounter through *Marvel Ultimate Alliance*. Doctor Doom is the final boss and you can actually pick all the Fantastic Four members for that showdown. You can alternate between Human Torch's fireballs, The Thing's rock fists, Invisible Woman's shields, and Mr. Fantastic's long-limbed attacks. It's up to you how the fight goes. You can even relive the battle in pinball form, thanks to the "Fantastic Four" pinball table in *Zen Pinball 2!*

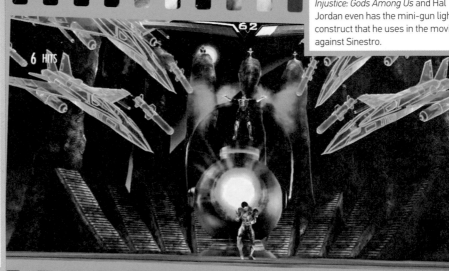

ANT-MAN
Zen Pinball 2

Although there are no *Ant-Man* games, you can come close to replicating the antics of the movie in *Zen Pinball 2*. The "Ant-Man" table has Hank Pym on standby, the lab from the movie, and Yellowjacket prowling in the middle. You can even activate the Pym Particle multiball, which sees tiny pinballs shoot around the table.

CAPTAIN AMERICA: CIVIL WAR
Ultimate Marvel vs. Capcom 3

The highlight of *Captain America: Civil War* is the big ruckus at the airport, which sees two opposing teams of super heroes come to blows over their beliefs. You can replicate some of this team battle in *Ultimate Marvel vs. Capcom 3*. You can pick Hawkeye and Captain America on the anti-registration side and have them go toe-to-toe with Iron Man and Spider-Man on the pro-registration side. You can even create your own dream team to fight alongside you in *Ultimate Marvel vs. Capcom 3*, teaming up with the likes of Ghost Rider or Wolverine, to give two examples. Best of all, you can combine all their attacks.

THE AVENGERS
LEGO MARVEL'S AVENGERS

LEGO *Marvel's Avengers* brings together moments from lots of Marvel movies with its own brand of humor. These are the very best of the bunch!

HELICARRIER HAVOC
Panic Stations

Remember in *The Avengers* when the Helicarrier, which serves as their headquarters in the sky, comes under attack? The "Helicarrier Havoc" level captures the action and excitement of this scene perfectly. From Bruce Banner losing control, to Captain America teaming up with Iron Man to save the Helicarrier from the resulting carnage, this level relives it all.

HELICARRIER HAVOC
Thor's imprisonment

There's a great scene in *The Avengers* when Loki tricks Thor into imprisoning himself. It's a dastardly moment of brother vs. brother in the movie and it's recreated in LEGO form, with lots of small embellishments and in-jokes that make the scene even funnier! Keep your eye on the background as the scene plays out . . .

RED HEAD DETENTION
Captain America vs. Red Skull

Captain America's cinematic journey kicked off with *The First Avenger* and the climax of the movie saw the super hero go up against Red Skull in a metallic, claustrophobic laboratory. The lab is a little bigger in "Red Head Detention," the LEGO *Marvel's Avengers* level that puts the two rivals on a collision course, but it's no less fun to play through.

Red Skull: It works. Power levels are stable.

SAND CENTRAL STATION
Spider-Man vs. Sandman

Spider-Man 3 sees Spidey up against Venom, Green Goblin, and Sandman. It's his battle against the latter that forms the first level of LEGO *Marvel's Avengers*, "Sand Central Station." As you battle against Sandman in his favorite forms, your nemesis grows in size. The battle eventually spills out of Grand Central Station and onto the streets of New York. Fortunately, unlike the movie, Spider-Man has back-up from Iron Man!

TAKING LIBERTIES
Fight on the Statue of Liberty

The climax of the first *X-Men* movie was a fight on the torch of the Statue of Liberty. What made the fight so much fun to watch wasn't just the unusual setting but also how each member of the team contributed to the fight. This has been recaptured perfectly with the "Taking Liberties" level in the LEGO game.

ULTRON UNDONE
Sokovia's sky fight

The climax of *Avengers: Age Of Ultron* sees The Avengers heading to the capital of Sokovia, where Ultron has built a machine that lifts part of the city into the sky. They have to evacuate the citizens, battle Ultron's sentries, and defeat Ultron himself. That's also your job in LEGO *Marvel's Avengers*. Unlike the movie, "Ultron Undone" has plenty of humor to keep the mood light during the intense action.

Quicksilver: This is S.H.I.E.L.D.?

THE EXPERT SAYS...

DARRAN JONES
Editor, Retro Gamer Magazine

The LEGO format has remained pretty much unchanged for about ten years now, but there's little sense in fixing something that clearly isn't broken. After all, LEGO games give you everything you'd want from a movie tie-in. Want to relive all the best bits from *Captain America: The Winter Solider*? You can do that in LEGO *Marvel's Avengers*. Want to battle The Joker and explore Gotham City? Then simply grab one of the LEGO *Batman* games. Loved *Guardians Of The Galaxy*? Then you *have* to play LEGO *Marvel Super Heroes*, which has all the characters available as unlockables. In fact, while I think about it, LEGO *Marvel Super Heroes* is probably still the best LEGO game. After all, where else can Spider-Man team up with Rocket Raccoon to save New York City?

STATS

9 gaming platforms for release

Over 200 playable characters

Over **100 characters** making their LEGO debut

8 different environments to explore

THE GREATEST MARVEL MASH-UP EVER?

LEGO MARVEL'S AVENGERS

⭐ **LEGO *Marvel's Avengers* is on a mission.** That mission is to please as many people as possible. It has classic LEGO gameplay, as you create teams with your favorite characters, find collectibles, solve puzzles, and build items with LEGO bricks. It has Marvel's greatest hits, borrowing from movies like *Captain America: The Winter Soldier* and *Iron Man*

3. It has a huge open world, allowing you to explore as much as you like. But what's really impressive are the touches that will resonate with all Marvel fans. Whether it's the debut of the Magneto Mobile, smashing Loki to the floor with Hulk, or unlocking some of the lesser-known heroes such as Howard The Duck, this game really hits the spot.

TIPS & TRICKS

★ FIND CHARACTER TOKENS
You'll unlock the option to buy new characters with studs but it's cheaper (and more fun) to try and find their hidden character unlock tokens instead.

★ REVISIT LEVELS
As you unlock new characters with unique powers, you'll be able to access new parts of old levels, so revisit them in Free Roam mode and explore!

★ HIGH SPEED
When visiting levels in Free Roam, pick a character who can fly (Iron Man) or who is fast (Speed) to make getting around faster.

TOP 5 SUPERPOWERS

ELECTRICITY

1 Heroes like Thor can command electricity, which makes them powerful combatants to have on the frontline of any battle. But electricity isn't just useful for shocking opponents—it can also power up generators, which is helpful for the many puzzles found throughout LEGO *Marvel's Avengers*.

REGENERATION

2 Ms. Marvel has one of the most useful powers of all the LEGO *Marvel's Avengers* cast when it comes to combat and it's not even electricity. Nor ice-beams. Nor any typical "offensive" power. It's regeneration! She slowly heals over time, which makes her a tough hero to beat in a fight.

STRENGTH

4 Hulk is well known in the Marvel universe for his brute strength. But it's not just fighting off the hordes of Ultron sentries, Chitauri, or other enemies that make his raw power so useful. Hulk can also smash through LEGO bricks no other character can, opening up secret areas and pathways.

ANT CONTROL

5 The coolest super power in LEGO *Marvel's Avengers* comes from Ant-Man. He controls ants and can use them to surround him like a shield or to capture enemies before making the swarms explode. With a mixture of defensive and attacking powers, Ant-Man is a great fit for any team.

FREEZE

3 Loki can create a freeze beam. This is useful in battle and also handy for turning objects into solid blocks of ice, to help reach secret areas. But more importantly, the freeze beam can also put out any fires blocking your path—which is essential, given the fiery carnage you have to fight through!

★ **MS. MARVEL WINS**
Once you've unlocked Ms. Marvel, use her for any tricky fights, as her Regeneration powers are incredibly useful. Aldrich Killian also has this power.

★ **EXPERIMENT!**
Try characters with different powers to see what their combat strengths are and also to see if you can unlock new areas. Don't stick to old favorites.

A huge Iron Man fan, Maggzy Cosplay shows off the armored concept version of the All-American hero

MAGGZY COSPLAY

WHO?
Kevin, aka Maggzy Cosplay, is a regular at conventions where cosplay features heavily. A huge Iron Man fan, his dream super hero game would be a first-person Iron Man game, with the full heads-up display from the inside of Iron Man's helmet, ideally made for virtual reality.

HOW?
So why did an Iron Man fan end up trying a Captain America cosplay? "I was stuck for ideas for my next cosplay, so I was just browsing through Google and Pinterest and came across a concept art for an armored Captain America," Kevin explains. "It was from this artwork that I then came up with my own armored version. The funny thing is I'm team Iron Man all the way, so Cap wouldn't have been my first choice."

COOLEST CHARACTERS

WENDIGO
This cursed monster knows how to get around LEGO *Marvel's Avengers* in style. He can bound on all fours, climb up the side of buildings, and even super jump into the air.

FIN FANG FOOM
Marvel's dragon is a formidable character when unlocked. He can pick up cars, shoot fireballs, breathe fire, grow to enormous size, and fly, making him useful for combat and exploration.

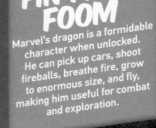

SQUIRREL GIRL

If you want to enjoy a different twist on LEGO Marvel's Avengers, try Squirrel Girl. She glides through the air, forms a shield of squirrels when she's in danger, and even throws squirrels to attack!

THE EXPERT SAYS...
DAN WEBB
Owner of XboxAchievements.com and PlaystationTrophies.org

LEGO Marvel's Avengers is TT Games' largest LEGO game yet, boasting a huge roster of characters cherry-picked from the entirety of Marvel's comic book history. While the main storyline deals purely with the events of several Marvel Cinematic Universe movies, the game's open-world hubs and bonus content feature a number of other popular Marvel faces, as well as a lot of more obscure ones, like Devil Dinosaur, Moon Boy and Butterball.

Most importantly, it retains TT's trademark LEGO gameplay that's consistently made the series a hit among loyal fans. It's got the puzzles, platforming, and collecting vast quantities of LEGO studs to unlock bonuses and secrets. LEGO games are always endlessly replayable, and LEGO Marvel's Avengers is yet another one. It's impossible not to love it.

DID YOU KNOW?

You can unlock the famous Lou Ferrigno version of Incredible Hulk from the 70s/80s TV shows, voiced by the actor himself.

SPEED

Blink and you'll miss him! Speed is so quick it's actually quite hard to control exactly where he's going. But that's exactly why he's one of the most fun characters to use in the game.

SUPER SKILLS

LEGO hosts the biggest Marvel party ever and every comic book fan is invited. Just make sure you're ready for the carnage!

| BRAVERY |
| MISCHIEF |
| DESTRUCTION |
| TEAMWORK |
| FUN FACTOR |

CREATE YOUR OWN HERO

DC UNIVERSE ONLINE

☆ **Have you ever wanted to create your own super hero? Well, that's exactly what *DC Universe Online* allows you to do.** Better still, you get to join in with the chaos and mayhem of DC Comic's finest characters. Pick your own look, fighting style, special powers, and even preferred method of travel (Flight? Running up buildings?) before plunging into the MMORPG fun. You can team up with other players or tackle missions solo, with mentoring from the likes of Superman, Wonder Woman, or Batman. Or if you fancy playing as a villain, you can work under the guidance of Lex Luthor, Joker, or Circe. With hundreds of missions, a massive city to explore, super hero vs. super hero battles, and its recent release on Xbox One joining PC and PS4, *DC Universe Online* is a game that never stops growing.

TIPS & TRICKS

★ KNOW YOUR RANGE
Your fighting style will either be effective up-close (Martial Arts, Shield, etc) or from range (Hand Blasters, Bow, etc). Remember this!

★ TOP UP POWER
If you're playing with the Mental, Gadgets, Munitions, Light, or Quantum power set, your job is to keep the other players powered up.

★ STICK WITH HEALERS
Players with the Water, Sorcery, Nature, Celestial, or Nature power sets are capable of healing. Stick close to these players.

TOP 5 MISSIONS

GREEN VS. YELLOW

Picking your way through Metropolis City Hall and battling the Yellow Lantern forces culminates in a huge showdown in the main hall itself. Sinestro and his force's appearance triggers an epic battle between the Green and Yellow Lanterns.

BANE BATTLE

2 When you finally corner Bane at the end of one of Batman's missions, it looks like a straightforward confrontation, until Bane balloons in size. Bane then causes the arena around him to crumble, so you have to dodge debris while fighting.

LUNATIC FRINGE

3 Harley Quinn has captured Robin, so you have to venture into the deep, dark depths of The Joker's Funhouse to save him. You need sharp wits and swift reactions to survive, as the funhouse is littered with traps that will catch out any unsuspecting hero.

SAVING RIDDLER

4 You need to find Riddler at the Monarch Playing Card Factory before Deathstroke tracks him down, but that means solving his riddles. It's not often you experience this in *DC Universe Online*, but when Deathstroke appears the action starts again!

AQUAMAN TURNS

5 Circe's forces have taken over the Condemned Shipping Office, leaving you to clear them out. But there's a surprise in the last room—Aquaman, who has been brainwashed by Circe into attacking you. Survive this battle and you'll feel as though you can survive anything in *DC Universe Online*.

★ CARRY SODAS
After each mission, go back to your safehouse and buy more sodas to top your health up during battle in emergency situations.

★ CHOOSE FLIGHT
Of all the travel methods, Flight is the most useful, as this allows you to hover near the ceiling during indoor battles and escape some attacks.

THE TOUGHEST BOSSES

With a simple pose and dramatic lighting, this is our favorite of Vavalika's Superman poses.

VAVALIKA

WHO?

This is an unusual twist on Superman cosplay! Female cosplayer Vavalika has decided to dress up as a female version of Superman, rather than cosplaying as Supergirl, to show her support for the Smallville super hero in response to the *Batman v Superman: Dawn Of Justice* movie.

HOW?

The Russian cosplayer has kept faithful to all the details of the iconic Superman look, even managing to pull off a feminine take on the trademark quiff. She's then posed for photos that recreate famous Superman comic book panels but our favorite has to be this simple portrait—classic, cool, and classy!

FULL HOUSE

This metal colossus guards the entrance to The Joker's Funhouse and has a variety of projectiles and close-range attacks.

SOLOMON GRUNDY

By himself, Solomon Grundy isn't too difficult, but he lurks near Poison Ivy's lair and hits you toward her deadly plants. Try to avoid him!

BIZARRO

Thanks to the range of his freeze vision and heat breath attacks, it's near impossible to escape battle against Bizarro once it's started. And Bizarro hits so hard, you'll want to run away almost immediately!

THE EXPERT SAYS...

RYAN KING

Games writer

I still remember that very first time I left the tiny starting hub of *DC Universe Online* and set foot in the sunny streets of Metropolis. A few cautious button presses in this strange new world and suddenly I was flying around the sky, looking down on the streets, buildings, parks, and other super heroes. It's so much fun soaring past the clouds, exploring anything and everything that piques your interest on the horizon. There hasn't been any moment in any other game that made me feel as heroic as the first time I saw a bunch of super heroes fighting Bizarro and I swooped in to join them. The camaraderie, the visual fireworks from each superhero's powers, the drama of the battle itself... it's simply incredible.

ARKILLO

This Yellow Lantern has an enormous pool of health and his range means you can't easily break away from battle once it's started. So, bring health sodas or a healing partner along before starting the showdown.

SUPER SKILLS

You can fly solo in *DC Universe Online* (literally!) but if you want to succeed then teamwork is key.

BRAVERY	
MISCHIEF	
DESTRUCTION	
TEAMWORK	
FUN FACTOR	

"DC UNIVERSE ONLINE IS A GAME THAT NEVER STOPS GROWING"

STATS ☰

5 super villains
to play as

4 districts
to unlock

28 the level needed
to unlock
Scarecrow

66 hideout tasks to
complete

340,435 YouTube
views for the iOS trailer

SEIZE CONTROL OF GOTHAM

BATMAN: ARKHAM UNDERWORLD

DID YOU KNOW?

This game is set before the events of *Batman: Arkham Asylum* and features all the characters and locations from that franchise.

⭐ A cool spin-off from Batman's console games, *Arkham Underworld* has you playing on the side of the villain. But you're not marching to the frontlines and taking on Batman in direct combat. Instead, this is about growing your criminal empire as you attempt to become the top boss in Gotham. You build a hideout, recruit henchmen, and complete missions to earn money and respect. Eventually, when you feel strong enough, you can raid hideouts of other online players and steal their loot. You also have to build your defenses to prevent your own empire from being raided. It's not long before Batman is the last thing on your mind, as you become embroiled in territory warfare with other players. This is a refreshing take on Batman's world and perfect for those who prefer using brains to brawn.

TIPS & TRICKS

⭐ **GET DAILY XP**
Make sure that you finish a raid with each super villain every day for a 300XP bonus. This will unlock new abilities over time.

⭐ **SEND IN THE BRAWN**
Make sure you send your strongest thugs to raid environments first. They will be able to weaken the enemies, allowing your weaker troops to succeed too.

MEET THE SUPER VILLAINS

THE RIDDLER

1 The Riddler is the default villainous character to play as in the game. He comes armed with the Question Arc, a melee weapon that fires an arc of electricity toward unsuspecting enemies and any objects that need destroying quickly, such as armaments and safes.

HARLEY QUINN

2 Harley is the first alternative super-villain that you unlock after completing a specific mission. In the heat of battle she can toss her unique Jack of Hearts weapon, a jack-in-the-box that wields dual machine guns. She's perfect for making short work of mob bosses!

KILLER CROC

5 The alter ego of sideshow wrestler Waylon Jones, Killer Croc is a dangerous, animalistic criminal with immense strength. If you need to bulldoze your way into an enemy hideout and take down defenses quickly, this super villain is the ideal choice.

MR. FREEZE

3 If you want to recruit someone who remains cool when things are hotting up, Mr. Freeze is your man. The second super villain you unlock, he has the ability to overcharge his suit, freezing anybody unfortunate enough to be standing in his blast radius.

SCARECROW

4 As the missions get increasingly demanding, especially on your human resources, you will want a leader who knows how to get into the minds of his enemies. This recruitable villain will pollute their brains with all manner of noxious chemicals. He scares a lot more than the crows!

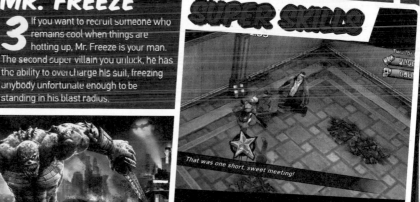

SUPER SKILLS

That was one short, sweet meeting!

Raid the hideouts of your underworld rivals to become the most powerful super villain in the whole of Gotham.

BRAVERY	
MISCHIEF	
DESTRUCTION	
TEAMWORK	
FUN FACTOR	

★ UPGRADE YOUR LAB
It pays to upgrade all aspects of your hideout over time, but upgrading the lab in particular unlocks new moves and tactics to use in your raids.

★ SCOUT WELL
When undertaking raids, scout out the locations first to establish the quickest and safest route to your objective.

HISTORY OF TEENAGE MUTANT NINJA TURTLES

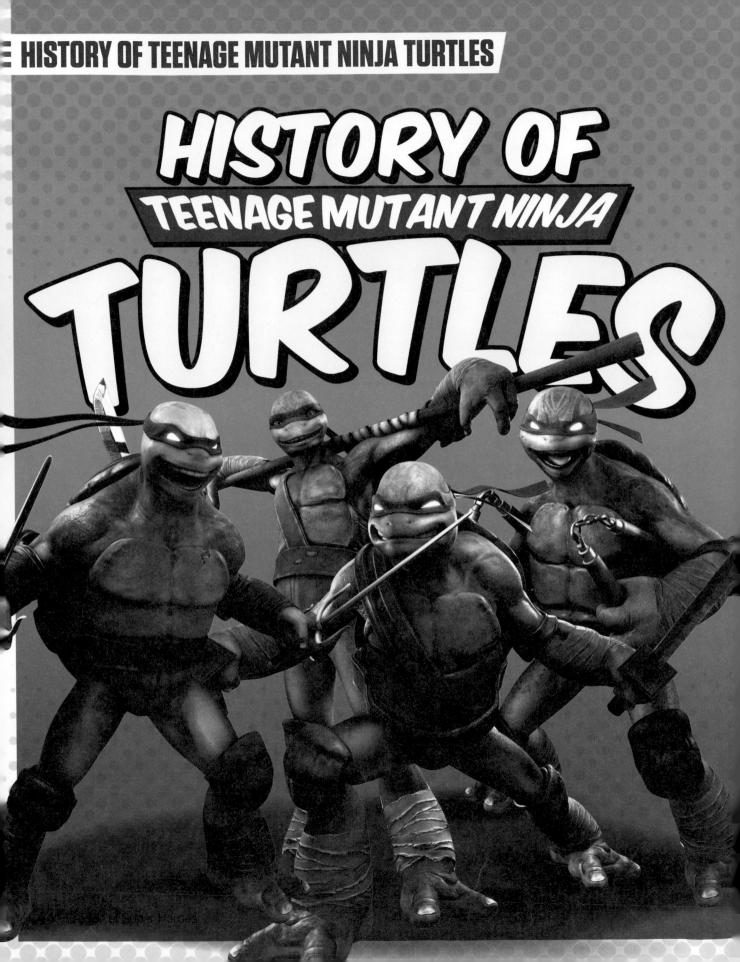

TEENAGE MUTANT NINJA TURTLES
NES

☆ This was the game that started it all and it is regarded as one of the best games ever made for Nintendo's first console, NES. *Teenage Mutant Ninja Turtles* was super difficult thanks to tricky platforming sections. It wasn't very well balanced either—the range of Donatello's staff made him the best Turtle, as he could attack safely from distance—but that didn't matter because we had a *Teenage Mutant Ninja Turtles* game.

1989

2007

TEENAGE MUTANT NINJA TURTLES
Xbox Live Arcade

☆ Making its debut in the arcades way back in 1989, the bright and buoyant *Teenage Mutant Ninja Turtles* has since been re-released on Xbox Live Arcade with a brand-new HD sheen, leaderboards, and online multiplayer . . . the latter being particularly useful given how difficult the game is! You have to defeat Bebop, Rocksteady, and Krang before taking on the mighty Shredder but it's the huge waves of Foot Clan you have to defeat along the way that will really test your survival skills.

TMNT
Xbox 360

☆ With night levels, muted colors, and comic-book panels telling the story, *TMNT* is a cooler, serious take on the gang's adventures. The co-op mode means you can tackle the game with a friend and fortunately, *TMNT* isn't anywhere near as difficult as older games in the series. So, you can focus on the fun to be had with the acrobatic combat and platforming as you leap around the rooftops, across rivers, and through the streets. In fact, anyone who wants an easy 1,000 Gamerscore should give this game a try, as the achievements are all straightforward to unlock.

2007

2009

TEENAGE MUTANT NINJA TURTLES: TURTLES IN TIME RE-SHELLED
Xbox Live Arcade, PSN

☆ This time-traveling adventure is an Xbox Live Arcade and PSN re-release of an old arcade classic, as the Turtles chase Shredder and Krang through the Wild West, the swashbuckling pirate era, and prehistoric times. With updated graphics and online co-op added to the original, this action game is simple to play. However, it's ridiculously good fun thanks to the strange and unfamiliar locations the Turtles find themselves in and the lightning-fast pace of the combat.

HISTORY OF TEENAGE MUTANT NINJA TURTLES

TEENAGE MUTANT NINJA TURTLES: SMASH-UP
Wii, PlayStation 2

⭐ Have you ever wanted to play a fighting game like *Super Smash Bros.* but with the characters from Turtles instead? That's what *Teenage Mutant Ninja Turtles: Smash-Up* delivered and it even had some of the developers from the famous *Super Smash Bros.* series working on it. Because it was a fighting game, *Smash-Up* had a huge range of characters, which meant while you could play as Leonardo and the gang, you also had the rare opportunity to play as the likes of April O'Neil, Nightwatcher, and Karai. You could even play as Shredder and see what it's like to take control of the Turtles' nemesis, for a change.

2013

2009

TEENAGE MUTANT NINJA TURTLES: OUT OF THE SHADOWS
Xbox Live Arcade, PSN, PC

⭐ This gritty take on the *Teenage Mutant Ninja Turtles* is as serious as you'll ever see the series get. The emphasis is on combat as you can counter attacks from enemies, upgrade attacks of your own, and have Donatello develop new weapons—at long last, Donatello really "does machines" as the famous intro song has always told us! *Out of the Shadows* is ideal for those who prefer the combat side of the Turtles over everything else.

TEENAGE MUTANT NINJA TURTLES
Xbox 360, Wii, 3DS

⭐ Based on the Nickelodeon series, this Turtles outing sees the group battling the Foot Clan and Krang across New York as they try and save April O'Neil from Shredder. Experts looking to get the most from the game have to find all 33 hidden ooze canisters, which let you upgrade your Turtle of choice. However, it's not necessary to complete the game as this is one of the easier games in the entire series, and even the final showdown against Shredder is surprisingly straightforward. Perhaps he wanted to take it easy for once!

2013

2014

TEENAGE MUTANT NINJA TURTLES **3DS**

⭐ Based on the 2014 movie, *Teenage Mutant Ninja Turtles* has almost every element of the series to date. You can collect materials to build new weapons, upgrade and unlock extra moves, you can even unlock talents unique to each character such as how Raphael can break through rocks and walls. Best of all is the look of the game—by copying the movie so closely, the Turtles wear the costumes they did for the big screen. They look their spectacular best as they spin and slice their way through the army of enemies before them.

Heroes

2014

2014

TEENAGE MUTANT NINJA TURTLES: TRAINING LAIR
Xbox Kinect

☆ One of the most unique *Teenage Mutant Ninja Turtles* games, this sees the Turtles' mentor, Splinter, training you . . . literally! You have to follow the ancient rat's sage-like commands and techniques in real life, as the Xbox's Kinect camera tracks your limb movement to see how well you're performing the moves. Unfortunately the game doesn't track some of the Turtles' moves that we're best at—reaching for pizza, mainly—but kung fu enthusiasts can work up a real sweat with this surprisingly fun game.

TEENAGE MUTANT NINJA TURTLES: DANGER OF THE OOZE
Xbox 360, PS3, 3DS

☆ Featuring a new, unique visual style, *Danger of the Ooze* is a 2-D platformer that sees you jumping upward and exploring as often as you do the traditional left-to-right route you usually see in the genre. With a few sneaky puzzles and a cool soundtrack, *Danger of the Ooze* isn't quite as frantic as some of the other games in the series, and can actually be enjoyed at a calm pace.

TEENAGE MUTANT NINJA TURTLES: PORTAL POWER
iOS, Android

☆ The gang take to iOS and Android for another game that sees you clearing the streets of bad guys, this time by drawing lines where you want the Turtles to attack. It seems easy at first but when the screen starts to fill up with enemies, it soon becomes a challenge to keep track of what's going on and where you should be attacking . . . this one is only for Turtle fans with incredibly quick reflexes and fingers fast enough to keep pace with the action!

2016

I, KICK, BATTLE

THE EXPERT SAYS...

LUKE ALBIGÉS
Editor, Play Magazine

The original *Turtles* arcade game from 1989 will always be a standout moment in the series for me, and playing it with three friends for the first time when I was a kid was an incredible experience. There was always an argument over who got to be which character (most of them ended up arguing over Michelangelo, which was fine by me as I wanted Donatello anyway!) Once you got into the game, it looked and sounded as close to the cartoon as games tech would allow at the time, and all while being an amazing co-op experience. As far as *TMNT* games go, this is still the one to beat for me. Turtle power!

STATS

1,300,000
views for the reveal trailer

4 players
can team up online

8 extra costumes
can be unlocked

BRING YOUR BUDS FOR CO-OP FUN

TMNT: MUTANTS IN MANHATTAN

DID YOU KNOW?
Developer Platinum Games also made the brilliant Transformers: Devastation and Legend of Korra.

⭐ The Teenage Mutant Ninja Turtles have been entertaining us for years with running battles against their nemesis Shredder, but the latest game, *Mutants in Manhattan,* is easily their best adventure yet. Four players can team up online as Leonardo, Donatello, Michelangelo, and Raphael, as they all use their unique skills from teleportation attacks to invisibility to cheerleading (honestly!) to slice and dice their way through the Foot Clan soldiers trying to conquer New York City.

What's really cool is that there's so much more to *Mutants in Manhattan* than just the combat. The acrobatic foursome can run up buildings, along walls and even parachute to the ground as they complete missions to tempt some of their notorious enemies out of hiding, from the hilariously incompetent Rocksteady and Bebop to the deadly Slash. Hilarious and heaving with missions to complete, this game is what every Turtles fan has been waiting for.

TIPS & TRICKS

★**STAY FOCUSED**
Try and eliminate single enemies at the start of the battle before others show up, so you can thin their ranks.

★**SWITCH CHARACTERS**
The biggest key to success is to rotate between each member of the group, using their skills to overwhelm the enemy.

PUNCH, KICK, BATTLE
WITH UNIQUE GROUP COMBAT CONTROLS!

★**SPECIAL SKILLS**
Leonardo's ability to slow down time should go first, then rotate through the other Turtles' skills.

MEET THE TURTLES

LEONARDO

1 Leonardo can use his ninjutsu skills to slow down time, a useful skill to survey the battlefield or squeeze in extra attacks, given how fast *Mutants in Manhattan* is. He can also join forces with another turtle to cut through the Foot Soldier ranks with ease, as they team up to unleash a devastating whirlwind attack.

DONATELLO

2 Donatello's best-looking skill is his barrage of teleportation attacks, which he can unleash in tandem with another member of the group. But his most important skill is his ability to throw pizza to fellow turtles, ensuring they keep their health topped up during battle.

What is it, Don?

MICHELANGELO

3 He's the most laidback member of the group and the one the others turn to if they need a morale boost. Michelangelo's main skill is cheerleading, which helps the other Turtles use their special skills more often. He can also mesmerize enemies with his dance moves!

SUPER SKILLS

Individually they're tough but together, the Teenage Mutant Ninja Turtles are practically unstoppable.

BRAVERY
MISCHIEF
DESTRUCTION
TEAMWORK
FUN FACTOR

★ REVIVING IS A PRIORITY

As soon as any Turtle falls in battle, make sure you revive them as a priority, even if you have to put yourself in a risky situation to do it.

RAPHAEL

4 Raphael can team up with another Turtle to create a huge shockwave that knocks enemies off their feet but his best skill is his most subtle—Raphael can turn invisible and sneak around the battlefield, looking for the perfect time to strike at unsuspecting members of the Foot Clan.

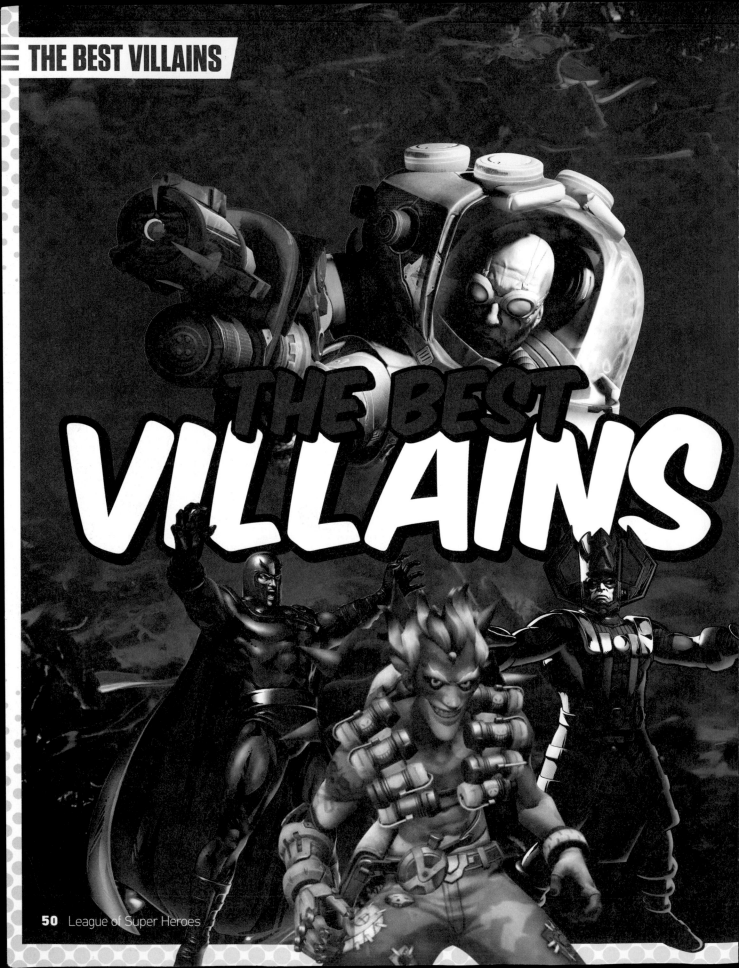

THE BEST VILLAINS

SENTINEL
(UNCANNY X-MEN: DAYS OF FUTURE PAST)

WHY?

As with the *Days of Future Past* comic, the storyline for the game sees Wolverine fighting an army of Sentinels, who have enslaved the United States. One gargantuan Sentinel would be enough but in this case, you're constantly under threat from several of them. Defeat one, and another quickly takes its place.

HOW TO DEFEAT HIM

In his most common form, Sentinel will stand in your way and stop you from progressing to the end of the level. He has two attacks—a chest burst that powers up (simply back away to avoid this) and energy orbs he fires from his hands (double-jump over these). In between these attacks, simply attack Sentinel's chest. When he fills up the screen, he has two further attacks—eye lasers (check where Sentinel is aiming and run in the opposite direction) and homing energy orbs (double-jump past them while running to the side of the screen). Again, attack his chest between these attacks to win.

THREAT

ALSO APPEARS IN . . .

MARVEL VS. CAPCOM 3

He was so powerful in *Marvel vs. Capcom 3* that the developers had to weaken him just a few months after the game came out. Even with that change, he remains a formidable foe.

Why do you laugh in the face of your own destruction?

What does Earth's Mightiest Heroe to one who rules the universe?

GALACTUS
ULTIMATE MARVEL VS. CAPCOM 3

WHY?

This is dramatic as villains get. In the comic universe, Galactus is the devourer of worlds, a gargantuan being said to be over 28 feet tall. In *Ultimate Marvel vs. Capcom 3*, he takes up the entire screen! There's no challenge like him in any fighting game. You can't jump over him, you can't throw him, and you can't bully him like you can other characters in *Ultimate Marvel vs. Capcom 3*. He's so powerful, he can even ignore the bulk of your attacks. Galactus truly is one of the most formidable opponents you'll ever face, in any game.

HOW TO DEFEAT HIM

Galactus is a huge target that's easy to damage, if you have a team that can attack from distance (characters like Nova, Iron Man or Hawkeye are great at this). You need to learn what attacks are coming from Galactus and how to defend against him. If he moves his hand back, start blocking, as he's going for a hand swipe. When he shouts "fall!" he's going to try and crush you with his hand, so rush toward him and the attack will hit behind you. When he takes a step back, he's going to slam his hands together along the ground, so jump to the top of the screen to avoid it. When he tries to flick you with his finger, jump away or block it. This attack can be particularly annoying because it'll flick your character out of the fight for a while, bringing one of your reserves in to take his place whether that's what you wanted to happen or not. The attack you can't avoid is when Galactus builds a huge ball of energy to slam it into the ground. Before he can build the energy ball, you need to do enough damage so the pain from your attacks stops him. It's a real war of attrition between your team and the devourer of worlds, but if you dodge enough of his attacks, you should triumph.

THREAT

JUNKRAT
OVERWATCH

WHY?

When the Australian Outback was turned into an irradiated wasteland following the explosion of a fusion core, a group of survivors known as Junkers formed a lawless society. Junkrat was one of them, scraping together metal and valuables from the ruins. The lingering radiation encouraged Junkrat's love for handling dangerous explosives and this spurred him on to an international crime spree with fellow Junkrat Roadhog. There aren't many villains in *Overwatch* and there certainly aren't any as unpredictable as Junkrat.

HOW TO DEFEAT HIM

Defeating Junkrat depends on the character you're using and who his teammates are, but the general tactics remain the same. Junkrat is weakest at long-range encounters, so that's where you want to be. His mines and steel traps are only a concern if you're close to him and his Total Mayhem trait can also be avoided by keeping your distance. The real threat is his Frag Launcher, but, when aimed, it gives you time to see the inbound frags. Simply move out of the way before they explode. His Rip Tire ultimate is an explosive tire that he can drive toward you, but you can shoot it from distance to safely detonate it.

THREAT

M.BISON
STREET FIGHTER V

WHY?

Ever since his debut in *Street Fighter II: The World Warrior*, Shadaloo leader M.Bison has stood tall as the arch villain in the series. In fact, he is one of the most notorious villains in gaming. Despite a tweaked moveset for *Street Fighter V*, and graying hair, he's still a formidable foe and his imposing presence is as terrifying as ever. His white eyes, his double-knee press, his evil laugh . . . this character is evil personified. The fact that he's got *Street Fighter V* characters F.A.N.G, Vega, and Balrog working for him, makes him even more dangerous.

HOW TO DEFEAT HIM

M.Bison's big weakness is that he can't defend himself when he gets up. While Ken and Ryu have their famous dragon punch to give themselves breathing space, and other characters like Zangief have command throws to ensure attackers keep their distance, M.Bison has limited options after he's knocked down. Matches against M.Bison are usually based on momentum—he has lots of fantastic attacking moves to keep you on the back foot but as soon as he's knocked down, he struggles to escape pressure. So stay on top of him when you knock him down, even something as simple as a sweep or a throw is far more valuable against M.Bison than it might be against others.

THREAT

MR. FREEZE
BATMAN: ARKHAM CITY

WHY?

As part of the chaos that's taken hold of Gotham, The Joker has kidnapped Mr. Freeze's wife, Nora. Batman is inflicted with a poison that Mr. Freeze holds the cure for but the ice-cold scientist won't hand it over unless Batman returns Nora, forcing them into a face-off. Batman has to quickly figure out how to defeat Mr. Freeze without being turned to ice by his ice gun and frost grenades. Mr. Freeze's suit also stops Batman's attacks and worse still, it will even scan the environment to find the caped crusader.

HOW TO DEFEAT HIM

This battle is widely regarded as one of the best boss battles in gaming, because it's a rare showdown where brain triumphs over brawn. Mr. Freeze adapts every time you successfully attack him, so you can't use the same method more than once. This just forces you to become creative. You can use Batman's takedowns that work so well through the rest of *Arkham City*, such as attacking from under grates and behind windows. But it's the smarter solutions that will really make the difference, such as electrifying puddles as Mr. Freeze walks over them or activating transformers so magnets pull in his metal suit, and the resulting slam injures the scientist. Eventually, Mr. Freeze gives up the battle and the vial, and even gives Batman the Freeze Blast gadget.

THREAT ✶✶✶✶✶

MAGNETO
X-MEN ARCADE

WHY?

Magneto is a force to be reckoned with in every game he appears in. His command of magnetic fields and his desire to see mutants become the dominant species often sees Magneto appearing as the final boss, and *X-Men Arcade* is no exception. But what makes this arcade appearance famous, and what was thankfully left untouched when *X-Men Arcade* was re-released for Xbox 360 and PSN, is a line of dialogue— "welcome to die." It's a mistranslation that has become legendary in gaming, especially as the line is delivered with Magneto's typical air of menace.

HOW TO DEFEAT HIM

Magneto has a series of deadly, hard-hitting attacks—a swipe with his hand when he gets too close, a repulsor blast if you roam too far, and a magnetic field that does damage. But he also has a big weakness, as his overconfidence means he will stop to laugh at you. This is when you strike!

THREAT ✶✶✶✶✶

CATWOMAN
DC UNIVERSE ONLINE

WHY?

Is she friend? Is she foe? In *DC Universe Online*, you work alongside Catwoman in "The Cat's Out The Bag." This mission involves helping the notorious thief place diamond eyes in ancient cat relics but unfortunately

this wakes the mystical powers inside the relic. They take control of Catwoman, and you're soon forced into battle against your former ally. The switch from fighting alongside Catwoman to confronting her is more effective because you've spent the entire mission seeing how she can handle herself in combat—and now, you have to survive her attacks! However, beware, she calls in tiger and panther cubs to help her.

HOW TO DEFEAT HER

Catwoman needs to be defeated nine times (she has nine lives like a cat) and this is her biggest weakness. After each "life," the relics call her back to recharge her, and this is your chance to use the health barrels dotted around the room to heal yourself, too. The biggest danger in this battle is accidentally smashing a health barrel in the heat of the action, so always watch where you're attacking, particularly if you're using a ranged character. If a tiger or panther cub is called in to help her, focus on them first and then turn your attention to Catwoman. When defeated, she'll say she owes you one of her nine lives before disappearing into the night.

ALSO APPEARED IN . . .

BATMAN: ARKHAM CITY

Is she friend or is she foe? It doesn't take long for *Catwoman* to appear in *Arkham City* but it does take a while to work our where her allegiances lie.

DID YOU KNOW?

You can actually play as Catwoman in *Batman: Arkham City*, as she has unique missions to complete in Gotham.

THREAT

MEET THE SUPERFANS

COSPLAY QUINTET

WHO?

The Cosplay Quintet is a group of amateur cosplayers, with a twist (and no, it's not that there are only four of them): Charlotte, Bea, Amy, Scarlett, and Annie (not pictured) have created female versions of famous male characters. "I chose to do a female version of Nightwing, the original Robin. He was originally just Batman's sidekick, but developed to become his own independent hero," says Amy.

WHY?

"We started cosplaying as it was a way of expressing our passion for comic books and movies, and the characters portrayed in them," says Charlotte, who cosplays as Lady Loki. "I enjoyed recreating this villain as she shows a strong female protagonist, and working on her with my friends is really what makes cosplaying so special to me."

4,710

Connect controller

SUPERMAN
LEGO BATMAN 3: BEYOND GOTHAM

DID YOU KNOW?

You can take control of Superman at any point in the game, so you'll know how tough he is by the time you come to fight him!

WHY?

"I told you we needed to worry about him going bad." Ominous words from Batman as Brainiac takes control of Superman, who has grown to gargantuan proportions following a Kryptonite mishap. Batman, Robin, The Flash, and Wonder Woman are then forced to figure out a way to stop Superman, who immediately turns on his former allies.

HOW TO DEFEAT HIM

The key is to survive until Superman's attacks start to bring down the arena around him. He has a ground pound, which causes the ground to spike up towards you, eye lasers, and super breath, which forces you to mash the buttons to cling onto the ground and avoid being blown away. Use The Flash to dodge his other attacks, as his speed makes it much easier for him to duck out of harm's way. When huge chunks of the arena fall down around you, smash them open and you'll see items that you can build. The first contraption you build is a sonic machine that directs bats toward Superman, the second is an electrical machine that requires The Flash's speed to power up. After taking hits from both of those machines, a cutscene is triggered when Batman appeals to Superman by calling him his friend, which sees Superman breaking Brainiac's mind control and returning back to normal.

THREAT

★ ★ ★ ★ ★

DR. DOOM
LEGO MARVEL SUPER HEROES

WHY?

It's no surprise that this notorious villain shows up during LEGO *Marvel Super Heroes*, given how he's tormented the Marvel universe over the years. In this game, Dr. Doom has hired villains to build the "Doom Ray Of Doom" to repel the threat of Galactus. However, the heroes don't trust him with that much power and try to stop him. Having already stopped Iron Man and Thor, it's up to Captain America, Storm, The Thing, and Spider-Man to put an end to Dr. Doom's mayhem.

HOW TO DEFEAT HIM

The first stage is to defeat the Doombots he sends after you. A counter at the top of the screen shows how many are left to be defeated. Then Dr. Doom sends a giant minion crashing into the fray. Step away from the minion's charge, jump on him with The Thing, and take his mask off. Then switch to Spider-Man to attach web to the minion's face and throw him out of the arena. Dr. Doom finally leaves the safety of his shield, jumping into a laser cannon to take shots at you. Build a patriotic panel for Captain America, then reflect Dr. Doom's laser beam at the spinning cylinders behind him. The explosion stuns Dr. Doom, so The Thing can land a free hit. Easy!

THREAT

MASTER CORE
SUPER SMASH BROS.

WHY?

After defeating the duo of Master Hand and Crazy Hand, you're then thrown into a fight against Master Core. This presents a challenge unlike anything else you'll have been up against in *Super Smash Bros.*! The first form is that of a giant man, who attacks from the side of the platform you're fighting on. Then Master Core turns into a strange, dinosaur-like creature, which joins you on the platform. After that, Master Core will turn into a series of swords to attack you, before finally taking on the form of a shadowy, larger version of the character you're playing as.

HOW TO DEFEAT HIM

When he's taken the form of a giant man, the main attacks you need to be careful for are the projectiles he fires (which explode in an outward "plus" shape) and his double swipe along the platform, which goes high and then low. When he joins you on the platform as a dinosaur-like creature, attack him from above, as this is the area he has the most trouble defending. The only attack he can hit you with when you're above him is leaping up into the air and summoning an electrical field around his body. As his sword form, the main attacks to worry about are the energy orbs and when he forms a sword formation of five around you—just look out for the glowing sword, which always attacks first. Finally, when Master Core becomes the mirror version of yourself, remember he has access to your strengths and weaknesses but as a bigger version of your character, he will have more range than you.

THREAT

BANE
INJUSTICE: GODS AMONG US

WHY?

A hulking mass of muscle and rage, Bane has no time or room for subtlety. He likes to stalk his opponents, bullying them into a corner with punches and powerful strikes, and knocking them back with bone-crushing throws when there's nowhere left to run. If that isn't scary enough, Bane can also inject himself with Venom to make himself even faster and stronger.

HOW TO DEFEAT HIM

Bane's powerful strength is balanced out by a crippling weakness. While Venom boosts his immense power, Bane's dependency on the mysterious chemical also leaves him weaker when it wears off. When fighting Bane, you need to keep a constant eye on his on-screen Venom meter. Play safe when he's powered up but when it wears off and Bane is weak, that's your time to pounce and turn the match in your favor.

THREAT
★ ★ ★ ★ ★

CHEF PEPPER JACK

SKYLANDERS TRAP TEAM

WHY?

Despite being freed from Cloudcracker Prison by Kaos, Chef Pepper Jack decides to side with the Golden Queen instead of his rescuer. His plan is to use Phoenix Chicken eggs to create an omelet of doom to blow up Skylands. The Skylanders take on Chef Pepper Jack, known for his explosive, fiery dishes, aboard his airship Chef Zeppelin, where the dastardly villain forces them to confront him in the ship's oven.

HOW TO DEFEAT HIM

Your main chance to damage Chef Pepper Jack is after he throws explosive peppers at you. They'll flash white and then blow up, covering the nearby area in scorching hot lava. Pepper Jack will charge at you through the fire and when he clatters into the wall, this is your chance to hurt him. He'll alternate these attacks with a laser grid, and some of these lasers require you to jump on the nearby steaks to stay safe. Pepper Jack will soon realize this and blow up the steaks, so be ready to jump off the steaks once the lasers have passed. There's no way you can rush this boss battle. You have to be patient and wait for the moments when you can attack him.

THREAT

STATS

700 **animations** for Batman's cape in *Arkham Asylum*

2 years is how long one person spent working on that cape

60 **people** worked on *Arkham Asylum*

440 Riddler challenges in *Arkham City*

THE HERO WE DESERVE

BATMAN: ARKHAM SERIES

⭐ **It's strange to think that *Batman: Arkham Asylum* actually opens with The Joker being captured.** Is this finally the end of his reign of terror, right as the game begins? Batman suspects otherwise but can't work out what's wrong. Then The Joker breaks free and lets the Arkham Asylum inmates out. And so the series begins as

Batman sneaks his way around The Joker's henchmen, takes on big names like Bane in bruising encounters, and glides through the intricate levels. The sequels up the ante by taking the mayhem from the asylum to the city. In *Batman: Return To Arkham*, Batman fans get to experience the chaos and bedlam of both the Asylum and Gotham once more.

TIPS & TRICKS

★ STAY UP HIGH
Whenever you enter a room, look high up for anything you can perch on like gargoyles or beams. This keeps you out of sight of guards.

★ DETECTIVE MODE
Use Detective Mode to spot guards but also to scan the room for any threats, such as mines, and glass windows you can smash through.

★ TAP THE BUTTONS
When in combat, it's tempting to hit the buttons quickly. Try to time button presses instead, so there's a calm rhythm to Batman's combat.

TOP 5 SHOWDOWNS

SCARECROW

1 Scarecrow relies on a series of fear-inducing toxins to weaken and harm his foes, and that presents Batman with a brand-new challenge. Scarecrow's influence is felt through *Asylum*, whether it's a hallway that warps and twists into a trip through Batman's haunted memories or the game pretending to crash. In the eventual showdown, you have to avoid Scarecrow's gaze as he continues to search for you in a nightmare world.

KILLER CROC

2 *Arkham Asylum* dips its toes into murky waters when Batman finds himself hunted in the sewers by Killer Croc, a mutant who tracks him by sound. Creeping along the floating boards in the sewers is painfully tense at times . . . it's a rare moment where Batman goes from the hunter to being the hunted.

BANE

3 When you fight Bane for the last time in *Arkham Origins*, it's a terrifying encounter, as Bane rips up grates and stomps through air vents trying to find you. Alfred warns you that Bane is becoming stronger as time passes, which puts more pressure on you to try and end the showdown quickly.

CLAYFACE

4 Joining the *Arkham City* fracas for what he calls "the performance of a lifetime," this monstrous mountain of mud is one of the more unusual foes Batman goes up against. Batman has to freeze Clayface to slow him down while dodging the mini Clayfaces who leap out and attack him.

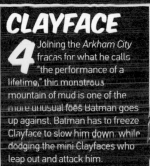

DEATHSTROKE

5 This showdown arrives early on in *Batman: Arkham Origins* but it's one of the coolest in the series, pitting Batman against an opponent who is his equal in hand-to-hand combat, determination, and gadgetry. This battle is between two martial artists at the peak of their powers and watching their flowing moves in action is awesome.

★ READY TO COUNTER
A small icon appears above enemy heads when they're about to attack, so make sure you press the counter button as soon as the icon appears.

★ TAKE OUT LONE GUARDS
If guards haven't noticed you yet, their patrols will see them eventually split up. Pounce on any guards who are walking around on their own.

The best thing about this costume? It's made to be worn, so it doesn't just look cool . . . you can actually feel like Batman wearing it, too.

JULIAN CHECKLEY

WHO?

Julian is the man behind Order 66, a company that creates costumes for movies and TV that's named after the famous *Star Wars* directive. As a huge Batman fan, Julian decided to make this Batsuit when he saw it in *Batman: Arkham Origins*.

HOW?

Julian worked with a company called Gauntlet FX to create the armor, then started trimming and sculpting the suit to get the Batman silhouette just right. The hardest part was making the suit look weathered. "The final result is a suit that looks like it has spent many nights on the streets of Gotham fighting bad guys," says Julian. Surprisingly, it's a lot more flexible to wear than it looks and Julian says it's one of the most comfortable costumes he's worn. He keeps it in storage, getting it out for for occasional charity or fan events.

COOLEST GADGETS

BATARANG
Batman's trademark batarang isn't too effective when it comes to dealing with any baddies in his way, but if he wants to hit a distant switch, it's perfect.

BATCLAW
The Batclaw can be used to pull winches or crumbling walls down to reveal hidden areas, but its best use is for grabbing weapons and pulling them right out of an enemy's hands.

SMOKE PELLETS

Smoke pellets are best used as a defensive measure should a guard with a gun spot Batman. They allow him to scramble to safety in the ensuing confusion.

DID YOU KNOW?

A lot of the photos scattered around the floor of Arkham Asylum are actually pictures of the developers.

LINE LAUNCHER

This gadget lets Batman connect a line between two high vantage points. Batman can then sneak along this high wire to reach new areas or take out guards.

THE EXPERT SAYS...

JON GORDON

Editor, games™

Before Rocksteady came along there was very little to celebrate when it came to Batman games. But with its *Arkham* titles it has managed to capture the essence of why I love the character and what I had always dreamed playing as him would feel like. These titles have been the ultimate super hero experience, giving us access to the full range of abilities that make Batman such a great hero. From using stealth to take down thugs and detective vision to hunt down clues, to swooping around a city and clearing out a street full of thieves with ease, the empowerment of the *Arkham* series of games has been amazing. And at the heart of it are the classic Batman and The Joker from the animated series, holding it all together and anchoring the whole series with a sense of familiarity. What a franchise.

SUPER SKILLS

He might work by himself but if there's an injustice that needs righting, Batman becomes an unstoppable machine.

BRAVERY	
MISCHIEF	
DESTRUCTION	
TEAMWORK	
FUN FACTOR	

HISTORY OF BATMAN GAMES

BATMAN: ARKHAM CITY LOCKDOWN
iOS, Android

☆ Despite its age, this game is still brilliant today, thanks to the great graphics and storyline. The bulk of *Arkham City Lockdown* is one-vs.-one fighting but it's broken up with lots of small distractions, such as Batman's batarang shootout, chasing goons down alleyways, and boss battles against the likes of Two-Face, Harley Quinn, and The Joker. The showdown against Solomon Grundy, where he chases Batman through a claustrophobic sewer, is particularly tense.

2011

THE DARK KNIGHT RISES
iOS, Android

☆ *The Dark Knight Rises* does an admirable job of squeezing Gotham into a mobile device. It shifts the focus away from one-vs.-one combat to exploring the city, swooping around as you find hideouts, follow targets, grapple hook on top of buildings, and silently eliminate guards. It's a serious take on the caped crusader's adventures that plays to the stealthy side of Batman as much as it does the all-out action, and that balance means *The Dark Knight Rises* offers something different to other *Batman* games.

2011

LEGO BATMAN 2: DC SUPER HEROES
iOS, Android, PS3, Xbox 360, Mac OS X, PC, Vita, 3DS, DS, Wii, Wii U

☆ *DC Super Heroes* opens with the "Man Of The Year" award, which is presented to Bruce Wayne with Lex Luthor as the runner-up. Then The Joker and his goons show up to steal the award, as he thinks he is the worthy winner. This triggers the hilarious events of LEGO *Batman 2*, which sees Batman and Superman doing battle with The Joker and Lex Luthor in Arkham Asylum, LexCorp, and even the Batcave. The highlight of this open-world adventure is doing battle with a giant, Joker-like robot . . . as if dealing with the ordinary Joker wasn't bad enough!

2012

2012

GOTHAM CITY IMPOSTORS
PC, Xbox 360, PS3

☆ *Gotham City Impostors* is what happens when you put *Overwatch*, Batman, and The Joker in a blender before standing well back from the noisy, explosive results. The idea is a strange one—one side is dressed as Batman, the other side dressed as The Joker in this outlandish team vs. team FPS showdown. You can change your look to be a muscular Batman on roller skates with a hunting bow, or a slimmer Batgirl with glider wings and a DIY rocket launcher. You can be whatever your imagination cooks up, a big part of *Impostors'* appeal. Better yet, it's now free to play on PC.

INJUSTICE: GODS AMONG US
PS3, Xbox 360, PC, iOS, Android, Wii U

☆ Batman and The Joker resume their long-running battle in this super hero brawl-fest, and this time, the caped crusader has brought his strongest gadgets with him. Batman can fire his grappling gun to hook opponents on the ground and in the air, throw batarangs from distance, chuck scatter bombs onto the ground while leaping to safety, and summon a swarm of bats around him for added defensive or offensive measures. His special move in *Injustice* is spectacular. He calls in the Batmobile to hit his opponent while back-flipping out of the way, proving he's a great driver, even when he's not actually behind the steering wheel!

2013

BATMAN: ARKHAM ORIGINS MOBILE
iOS, Android

☆ Unlike the console version, the mobile take on *Batman: Arkham Origins* is a one-vs.-one fighting game, where you tap and swipe to perform attacks with Batman. The trick is to know when to switch between your assault stance, which does more damage to your foes, and your defensive stance, which sacrifices damaging attacks for a chance to heal yourself. With each victory you can upgrade your Batsuit and you'll even get the chance to discover entirely new Batsuits to wear. Fast, frantic, and furious, this is the sort of game you'd imagine Batman might play in his rare downtime.

SCRIBBLENAUTS UNMASKED: A DC COMICS ADVENTURE
Wii U, 3DS, PC

☆ You might be playing as *Scribblenauts*'s hero Maxwell rather than Batman in *A DC Comics Adventure* but that doesn't mean the caped crusader doesn't feature in the fun. Maxwell can summon Batman to join the fight and best of all, as part of the DC 2000 characters in this *Scribblenauts* outing, there are plenty of costumes variations you can choose from, too. You can summon Bruce Wayne (who's dressed as a private eye), Batman imposter Hush, and even a pirate version of Batman. It's like a party by Batman fans, for Batman fans, where everyone is trying to outdo each other with their costumes!

2013

BATMAN

OF ZUR-EN-A

2013

2015

LEGO DIMENSIONS
PS4, Xbox One, Wii U, PS3, Xbox 360

This comedic take on our favorite super heroes sees Batman teaming up with Gandalf from *Lord of the Rings* and Wyldstyle from *The LEGO Movie*, as they try to stop Lord Vortech from conquering the LEGO Multiverse. Batman is equipped with his trademark batarang, a grapple hook, and, if the odds aren't looking too favorable for our hero, a nifty stealth move. Best of all, Batman is equipped with something we're not used to seeing from him—a snappy one-liner! This is the funniest version of Batman to date, and it's worth playing just to see Batman in this fine form.

BATMAN V SUPERMAN WHO WILL WIN
iOS, Android

Despite the promise of the title, this doesn't actually see Batman and Superman go head to head. Instead, you get to choose which of the two heroes you want to play as in an endless runner, as you collect icons and try to survive for as long as possible to grab a high-ranking score. You can jump in the Batmobile and even collect temporary shields for Batman as you race through the streets of Gotham—just don't expect Batman and Superman to get into an actual fight!

2016

2016

BATMAN: RETURN TO ARKHAM
Xbox One, PS4

⭐ This remastered collection gives you the chance to play through two of the best Batman games ever made. First, you'll be tasked with exploring Arkham Asylum to stop The Joker's dastardly plot. Then, once you've crept through narrow corridors and swung through large laboratories, you can explore Arkham City. These two games make you feel like you really are Batman, and that's all we've ever wanted. Gliding across the city feels incredible, and as you swoop around you'll soon see why these games were so loved when they were originally released.

THE EXPERT SAYS...

SIMON MILLER

Head of video production, Videogamer.com

While it's easy to appreciate all super heroes, Batman is more relatable because he's someone who doesn't have powers. All it really takes to be The Dark Knight is lots of money, some gadgets, and a friendly butler called Alfred. And, of course, years of training . . . This is why *Batman* video games are so good, though—you can just forget you're playing a game and buy into what's happening on the screen. On top of that, who doesn't want to drive the Batmobile, or fly over Gotham City at night? The *Arkham* series lets you do all of that and more. They're perfect!

THE COOLEST SUPER HERO CAMEOS

CAMEOS ARE REWARDS FOR DEDICATED AND EAGLE-EYED PLAYERS, AS THEY GET TO GLIMPSE OTHER COMIC BOOK HEROES SNEAKING INTO THE GAME.

ULTIMATE MARVEL VS. CAPCOM 3

Capcom's three-vs.-three fighting game is packed with cameo appearances, which all pop up in the endings for different characters

> Chris Redfield's ending gives us a rare glimpse of Matt Murdock the attorney at work—the alter ego of crime-fighting super hero Daredevil.

MATT MURDOCK

...and furthermore, I will present incontrovertible evidence of the defendant's involvement with the Raccoon City Incident of 1998.

DAREDEVIL

> Capcom's knight in shining armor, Arthur, ends the game by squaring up to his biggest battle yet Fin Fang Foom! The legendary dragon lurks menacingly, while Arthur saves the princess.

> Kingpin's long and harsh reign as a New York crimelord is finally over as Chun-Li brings the notorious criminal to justice in her ending.

FIN FANG FOOM

> The most glamorous of all the X-Men, Dazzler can be seen sharing the ending and hitting the stage with Capcom's cat-girl Felicia.

DAZZLER

KINGPIN

The grotesque Mojo and multi-limbed Spiral are usually involved in serious Marvel storylines ... so it's nice to see them turning to comedy for Viewtiful Joe's ending!

Popular hero Nightcrawler appears in more movies than he does games, so it's nice to see the teleporting mutant show up in Trish's ending.

MOJO

I told him over and over and over and over and over again! Do NOT ad lib your lines! I could just murder someone, you know?

MOJO, SPIRAL

NIGHTCRAWLER

For the last time, I am not a demon!

NIGHTCRAWLER

Silver Surfer is one of the most powerful super heroes around and when you complete the game with Zero, you get to see him comparing the worlds of Marvel and Capcom.

Ghost Rider's ending shows him getting his hands on his nemesis Mephisto. It's one of the rare times you can see Mephisto captured with no easy way out.

SILVER SURFER

Perplexing indeed. I cannot tell the difference between any of these worlds.

GHOST RIDER

Wouldn't you agree, Mephisto?

SILVER SURFER

MEPHISTO

After defeating Galactus, Capcom's ninja Strider finally finds a worthy opponent in his ending, as he squares off against Marvel's Lady Deathstrike.

JILL

And I thought I had it bad when had to worry about fighting zom

Capcom's zombie-slayer Jill teams up with Marvel's vampire-hunter Blade in her ending, as they're both surrounded by creatures of the night. It's the first time the two characters have ever joined forces.

BLADE

LADY DEATHSTRIKE

...!?

LADY DEATHSTRIKE

Have you ever wondered why some of the characters from Marvel vs. Capcom 2 didn't make it into the sequel? A poster on the background of the slums stage explains their fate. Gambit, Psylocke, and Colossus were apprehended while Cable, Marrow, and Ice-Man were slain.

On the New York stage, you might catch a glimpse of a helicopter flying around in the background . . . with none other than Peter Parker's boss, Jonah J. Jameson, hanging out the side with a camera in hand.

GAMBIT, PSYLOCKE, CABLE, AND OTHERS

J. JONAH JAMESON

Marvel legend Stan Lee makes cameo appearances in almost every Marvel movie, so it's fitting that he makes cameo appearances in LEGO Marvel's Avengers as well. In fact, he makes 35 appearances throughout and if you find them all, you also unlock a Trophy or Achievement, depending on the console you're using.

THE AMAZING SPIDER-MAN 2

In a scene that plays after the credits, super villain Chameleon emerges in Kingpin's office, removing his mask. It turns out that Chameleon had disguised himself as Norman Osborn's personal assistant, Donald Menken, fooling Spider-Man earlier in the game.

Fisk: Now... the real work begins.

CHAMELEON

LEGO MARVEL'S AVENGERS

STAN LEE

You can hear the roving reporter crying for help in the level "Painting The Town Black." She's trapped in a burning building behind some glass. You don't even need to use Superman to save her! All you need is a character with the ability to shatter glass.

Here's an interesting cameo that has been under Marvel Avengers Academy players' noses ever since launch, and they might not have even realized. The Hulk is voiced by none other than WWE wrestler, John Cena!

Lois Lane Rescued!

LEGO DIMENSIONS

MARVEL AVENGERS ACADEMY

LOIS LANE

JOHN CENA

In a world of super heroes, it was a surprise to see talk show host Conan O'Brien show up in LEGO Batman 3. It seems as though his only superpower in the game is that he never stops talking!

LEGO BATMAN 3

CONAN O'BRIEN

He's tucked away in the cell behind the courtroom, surrounded by calendars and marked dates. Visit him on a special date such as New Year's Day and he'll have something new to say to Batman. Visit him on enough special dates and he'll eventually break free.

BATMAN: ARKHAM CITY

CALENDAR MAN

He might be known as Captain America's nemesis but Red Skull's role in *Super Soldier* is that of a minor cameo in the game's ending. After Captain America destroys the Sleeper, Red Skull shows up to survey the wreckage and tell Armin Zola to get back to work.

CAPTAIN AMERICA: SUPER SOLDIER

RED SKULL

This impish creature has been part of a *DC Universe Online* seasonal event, the aptly-named Mxyzptlk's Mischief. But lucky players can bump into him flying high over the streets of Metropolis, offering unique quests to curious heroes.

DC UNIVERSE ONLINE

MISTER MXYZPTLK

INJUSTICE: GODS AMONG US

There are a wealth of cameos sprinkled throughout *Injustice*. Here are some of our favorites...

Green Arrow's nemesis shows up in the S.T.A.R. Lab missions, dressed as Green Arrow! Hit Merlyn with arrows shot from distance to defeat him.

During his S.T.A.R. Labs missions, Sinestro has to overcome Green Lantern. In the background of the final level, you'll see Atrocitus, a member of the Red Lantern Corps. He's also a playable character in *Injustice 2!*

MERLYN

ATROCITUS

Take a guess at who shows up in the Harley Quinn S.T.A.R. Labs mission called "Two-Face"? Harvey Dent is in the background of the battle against Catwoman, flipping a coin to determine who he is going to attack next.

The Joker wants to steal Lex Luthor's nanobot technology ...and calls on the Atom to do it for him. By shrinking himself down, Atom can dodge past Luthor's security. This is one of the rare instances where you get to play as a cameo character.

ATOM

TWO-FACE

Giganta can be seen in the background of the Hall of Justice level, doing battle with Atom. Better yet, you can hit your opponent into Giganta, who takes offense and then throws your foe straight into the Hall of Justice itself!

Raven's father appears during her super move. Raven transports her opponent to another realm, where she hits them with a series of quick attacks, then Trigon appears and blasts them away with a beam from his eyes.

GIGANTA

TRIGON

STATS

Five playable Transformers

7 chapters

1,700,00 YouTube views for launch trailer

3 new weapons added after release

ROBOTS IN DISGUISE

TRANSFORMERS: DEVASTATION

DID YOU KNOW?

The final difficulty you unlock is called Magnus. This turns Devastation into one of the hardest games ever made!

☆ **You can't get much cooler than a robot that can turn into a vehicle whenever it wants to.** So, it's no wonder that the clash between the friendly Autobots and evil Decepticons has been so entertaining—as towering robots pit their immense power and super speed against each other in epic battles. With Decepticons launching another plan to take over Earth, you have to choose your favorite Autobot and try to stop them. You can use melee attacks, ranged attacks, and transform into a vehicle to drive straight into your foe. You can also build new weapons with the parts you collect from each mission, essential for your showdowns against Decepticons such as Shockwave, Starscream, or even Megatron! *Devastation* isn't just for Transformers fans, any action game fan will love this, too.

TIPS & TRICKS

★ **STAY CLOSE**
You should stay close to your opponents and use melee attacks to do the most damage. If they are at distance, use projectile attacks while closing the gap.

★ **SLOW DOWN TIME**
Try to dodge attacks rather than avoiding them. Successfully dodging attacks will slow down time, making it easier to strike back.

OPTIMUS PRIME

1 The Autobots' leader has a powerful cannon, devastating uppercuts, and an energy sword that allows him to cut through enemies with ease. Best of all, when you switch him to vehicle mode, Optimus Prime transforms into his trademark truck and smashes through anyone or anything standing in his way!

BUMBLEBEE

2 This nimble Autobot doesn't look too threatening. He's small, bright yellow, and transforms into a mini car. But, beware, if Bumblebee gets close, he has awesome punching attacks and can even launch into a shoulder charge straight out of his mini form. Watch out Decepticons!

SIDESWIPE

3 Sideswipe is the Autobot of choice for those who want to wreak havoc with style. He's equipped with an energy sword, flare gun, and missiles. Sideswipe also has an incredibly fast punch rush that leaves opponents scrambling to get away. Best of all, in his stylish vehicle mode, Sideswipe transforms into a slick sports car.

WHEELJACK

4 With his long, spindly limbs, Wheeljack has reach the other Autobots can't match. He's a little slower than his Autobot allies, though, making him difficult to master. It's worth persisting with Wheeljack though, as his long reach makes him a good choice for some of the trickier boss battles.

(While Moving - Dino Mode)
[O] (Tap Quickly) Run

GRIMLOCK

5 Last, but not least, this is the coolest Autobot of them all. Rather than transforming into a vehicle, Grimlock transforms into a T-rex! As a dinosaur, Grimlock can roll away from danger and breathe fire. He can even swipe with his tiny limbs, although it's more likely to make your opponent laugh than do too much damage.

SUPER SKILLS

It's the classic Autobots versus Decepticons battle in gaming form . . . and as always, teamwork is the key.

BRAVERY	
MISCHIEF	
DESTRUCTION	
TEAMWORK	
FUN FACTOR	

★ **CREATE BREATHING SPACE**
If you're taken a lot of damage, enter vehicle mode and retreat! Use this time to launch your next attack as your opponent chases you and regain the initiative.

★ **LEARN COMBOS**
There are lots of easy combos to learn and these are the best way of doing damage. Check the pause menu to find your character's best combos.

STATS ≡

22 playable characters in *Marvel Ultimate Alliance*

8 downloadable characters in *Marvel Ultimate Alliance*

53 bosses to battle in *Marvel Ultimate Alliance 2*

34 playable characters in *Marvel Ultimate Alliance 2*

THE ULTIMATE TEAM-UP

MARVEL ULTIMATE ALLIANCE SERIES

DID YOU KNOW?

Marvel announced Spider-Man's Aunt May as a playable character in Marvel Ultimate Alliance 2 ... but it was an April Fool's joke!

☆ **The premise behind *Marvel Ultimate Alliance* and its sequel is simple.** Choose a team of four super heroes, leap into action, and use your superpowers to destroy your enemies. Both *Marvel Ultimate Alliance* outings are overhead action games that see you tackling an army of villains. However, you won't win unless you build the right team. Each super hero has unique powers and works with allies in different ways. Iron Man's Unibeam is a devastating long-range attack but when reflected off Captain America's shield, it does even more damage. Hulk lacks long-range attacks but he can throw Psylocke at his foes. Finding the right combinations with your friends is where the fun in *Marvel Ultimate Alliance* lies. And if you want a break from the action, there's an in-game Marvel quiz, catering to all levels of comic book fandom.

TIPS & TRICKS

★ TEAM UP
In *Marvel Ultimate Alliance*, you gain a bonus if your group of four is a known "team" such as the Avengers, Fantastic Four, or X-Men.

★ FOCUS ON ONE POWER
You'll have a variety of superpowers to upgrade as you level up but focus on making one superpower stronger than the others, and make this your main attack.

★ SILVER SURFER AND FRIENDS
The strongest characters in *Marvel Ultimate Alliance* are Silver Surfer, Human Torch, Sabretooth, and Mr. Fantastic.

TOP 5 CHARACTERS

IRON MAN

1 The best thing about Iron Man is how well he works with others. He can fire his Unibeam into Storm's tornados to power them up, hurl pulse bombs for Wolverine to chuck at enemies, and blast foes grouped up by Magneto's magnetic powers. Whatever the group, Iron Man has a creative way to team up with them!

IRON FIST

2 While these games tend to tilt towards explosive actions, it's refreshing to have heroes who do something different. Iron Fist is a martial arts expert but he can also help by healing his allies. He adds a different flavor to combat scenarios as he looks to mend his teammates' wounds rather than weaken his enemies.

SPIDER-WOMAN

3 Spider-Woman has tools for every job. She has a bioelectric beam, traps, and bouncing projectiles. She can also reach the farthest corners of the screen with her attacks. Best of all is her Attract special move. This causes all enemies to focus on her while she gives herself a defensive boost. This gives your team valuable breathing space.

SPIDER-MAN

4 If the pace of the combat is too much, Spider-Man is the hero to slow things down with his various web attacks and trademark Spidey Sense. His best attack is Bungee Bash, where he'll grab all the enemies before him and quickly spin them up into helpless web sacks. Not only it is useful, it's incredibly fun to watch.

WAR MACHINE

5 You might not play as him but the boss battle against pro-registration War Machine in *Marvel Ultimate Alliance 2* shows off how well-designed he is. He can attack with his steel fists up close, fire missiles from distance, and use his rocket boosters to get close. You have to stay on your toes and keep moving to survive.

SUPER SKILLS

Four super heroes, all displaying their awesome superpowers at the same time. What's not to love?

- BRAVERY
- MISCHIEF
- DESTRUCTION
- TEAMWORK
- FUN FACTOR

★ THOR LEADS THE WAY

The strongest characters in *Marvel Ultimate Alliance 2* are Thor, Song Bird, and Nick Fury. They can do the most damage in the shortest space of time.

★ KNOW WHO TO AVOID

The weakest characters in *Marvel Ultimate Alliance 2* are Daredevil and Mr. Fantastic, who struggle to reach the damage output of other characters.

DOES WHATEVER A SPIDER CAN

SPIDER-MAN UNLIMITED

You might think of endless runner games as simple high-scores chases, but think again. Spider-Man's first-ever take on the popular genre is crammed with bonuses and extras you wouldn't normally find in endless runners. There's a fully-fleshed out storyline, as the Sinister Six return, boss battles to fight, and secret areas to discover. This endless runner even takes flight, as Spider-Man leaves the ground to swing through the skies of New York City and climb up the sides of buildings. You'll need your spider-sense to be tingling to guide the famous web-slinger out of harm's way, especially as the game accelerates to eye-watering levels of speed. Can you keep up?

+ 20

5 COMBO

DID YOU KNOW?

Spider-Man Unlimited doesn't just have online leaderboards for the world —it tells you how you compare to everyone in your area.

SUPER SKILLS

+ 40

2 COMBO PRECISION

With his gymnastic moves, Spider-Man has everything he needs to keep up with the lightning-fast chaos of *Unlimited*.

| BRAVERY |
| MISCHIEF |
| DESTRUCTION |
| TEAMWORK |
| FUN FACTOR |

TIPS & TRICKS

★**NO DISTRACTIONS**
The calmer the environment you play in, the better. *Spider-Man Unlimited* demands a lot of focus and concentration if you want to do well.

★**MOVE EARLY**
As the levels speed up, adjust your tactics. Try to dodge obstacles and attacks as early as possible, to stay safe.

★**DON'T TAKE RISKS**
Don't insert yourself into dangerous high-score routes if you're not confident you'll survive. Always play safe.

GOOD!
0 4 HITS

DID YOU KNOW?
Developer Gameloft also makes the award-winning Asphalt racing series.

HAMMER TIME

THOR: THE DARK WORLD

⭐ He might be one of the most powerful beings in the universe but even Thor sometimes needs help. Wielding legendary hammer Mjolnir isn't enough to keep the evil Malekith and his horde of Dark Elves at bay in this action-adventure. While playing as Thor and using the power of lightning and Mjolnir to do battle, you can summon allies to fight alongside you. They free captives, fire arrows at distant threats, and protect you with their sword. These loyal soldiers make you feel like a commander on a battlefield. You can even be sneaky and take a step back from the action, watching your forces take on the Dark Elves as the chaotic spectacle unfolds.

SUPER SKILLS

With the mighty Mjolnir and his loyal friends by his side, Thor has everything he needs to face his biggest challenge yet.

BRAVERY	
MISCHIEF	
DESTRUCTION	
TEAMWORK	
FUN FACTOR	

TIPS & TRICKS

★ CALL YOUR ALLIES
Get in the habit of calling in the Einherjar—Thor's allies—whenever the meter at the bottom of the screen isn't full.

SEASON REWARD

★ LEVEL UP
Always focus on leveling up the health of your Einherjar, as allies with a large pool of health will become really valuable.

★ BUY GOLDEN ARMOR
This is one of the earliest upgrades you can get for Thor and one of the most important, as it stops Thor from taking fire damage.

OCTODAD

SEEN IN:

Octodad: Dadliest Catch

SUPERPOWERS:

Master of disguise

You might not think that Octodad is a super hero, but have you ever tried to do the shopping using just your arms? Octodad has disguised himself as a human, but being an octopus, he's not the best when it comes to household chores, which almost gives his secret away. Whether it's stomping spiders in the bedroom to keep the family calm or mopping the floor in the kitchen to tidy up mess, the ordinary becomes the hilarious as Octodad slips and slides around, causing chaos wherever he goes.

Octodad's trying to blend in and the suit helps him stay hidden ... but his clumsy antics often give him away.

Octodad needs to evade the suspicion of his wife, Scarlet, who is alarmed by her husband's odd behavior.

JOE DANGER

Joe Danger's look is inspired by the most famous stuntman of all time, Evel Knievel.

SEEN IN:

Joe Danger, Joe Danger 2: The Movie, Joe Danger Infinity

SUPERPOWERS:

Defying gravity

Joe Danger isn't just any ordinary stuntman. He can leap higher and farther than you can believe and some of the risks he takes will make your jaw drop! Whether he's on the back of his trademark motorbike, riding skis, or even using a jetpack, Joe Danger races through a series of gravity-defying stunts. Points are awarded for how quickly he completes the course and for the difficulty of the stunts executed along the way. He's the super hero we all want to be!

Joe Danger wears a cape to make his airborne tricks look even more dramatic.

SPELUNKY GUY

Some caverns are pitch black and Spelunky Guy needs to carry a torch with him. Just be careful not to drop it or go swimming with it!

Spelunky Guy's collection of ropes allows him to descend safely to the lower depths of the caverns.

SEEN IN:
Spelunky

SUPERPOWERS:
Deep pockets, defeating monsters

Like a miniature Indiana Jones, Spelunky Guy heads to ruins and historical sites in an attempt to unearth mythical treasures. He collects a range of items, from compasses to sticky gloves to capes to help him, as he works his way through a series of increasingly treacherous caverns. What initially seems like a treasure-collecting jaunt opens up into a bigger adventure, as you realize you can save damsels in distress, find hidden caves, and even take on legendary monsters. He might be small, but there's no denying the size of Spelunky Guy's heart.

SHOVEL KNIGHT

SEEN IN:
Shovel Knight

SUPERPOWERS:
Shovel mastery

He looks like any other knight but he's not armed with a sword and shield, or any other of the medieval weaponry you might expect. No, our hero chooses to march into battle with a shovel. He hits enemies out of the way with the shovel, bounces on it, and uses it to dig hidden power-ups out of the ground. Shovel Knight doesn't just limit himself to his trusty spade either, as he collects other unusual weapons such as a Flare Wand, War Horn, and Throwing Anchor. He's a bit strange but mightily effective!

Whether it's digging up objects or bouncing on enemies, Shovel Knight is nothing without his trusty shovel.

The Shovel Knight amiibo is the first by Nintendo that allows you to scan the code without removing the figurine from its packaging.

THE EXPERT SAYS...

PAUL WALKER-EMIG
Writer, nowgamer.com

Yes, Shovel Knight is a pretty weird hero. You don't often see a person, clad head to toe in medieval armor, beating up angry snakes with a shovel, right? But somehow, in this game, it all works perfectly. The graphics might not be up to the standards that modern gamers have come to expect, but every character is carefully crafted, and every level is designed specifically to test your platforming skills.

While other classic games from names like Mario, Sonic, and Rayman have updated their look and feel to match modern gaming expectations, *Shovel Knight* does the opposite. This is a modern gem, hidden under retro wrapping, and anyone who calls themself a gamer should play it right now.

MAXWELL

SEEN IN:

Scribblenauts, Super Scribblenauts, Scribblenauts Remix, Scribblenauts Unlimited

SUPERPOWERS:

Creating anything you type

Maxwell is blessed with perhaps the coolest and most useful superpower of anyone in this book—he'll bring to life anything that you type. Type "ladder" and he'll conjure up a ladder to help you reach higher places. Need to fill a gap? Type "rock" so Maxwell will magic a rock into existence for you to use. Love dinosaurs, and also love robots? Type in "Robot T-Rex" and you'll get a giant mechanical dino that you can ride around the level—it's that combination of your creativity and Maxwell's powers that makes *Scribblenauts* a joy

> Maxwell has to collect "Starites" to complete each level, but most are just out of reach, that's when you need to think of what object to conjure.

> There are over 10,000 objects you can conjure using Maxwell's notepad. Getting them all would take hours!

WONDERFUL 101

SEEN IN:

The Wonderful 101

SUPERPOWERS:

Teamwork, forming cool weapons

Here's teamwork at its best. By combining their powers, *The Wonderful 101* can conjure up all sorts of oversized weaponry to squash their enemies. When Red is in charge of the crew, they can form a gigantic flaming fist. With other colors of hero in charge of the group, the weapons available include claws, whips, and cannons. These weapons aren't just used for attacking enemies either. The giant fist can be used to pull huge crates toward you so that you are able to leap onto higher platforms, the whip can be used to connect moving trains, and so on!

> Switching leaders is the key to *The Wonderful 101's* power. If you need to cut a chain, then use Blue's sword to slice through it.

> The leader of the group determines the weapon that's formed when the members join forces—if Red is in charge, it's a flaming fist.

On his quest for treasure, Captain Toad has to visit some dark, dingy caverns ... fortunately he's brought his flashlight with him so he can always see where he's going!

Without agility on his side, Captain Toad has to use his pickax to clear away obstacles, which leaves him vulnerable to attack from nearby enemies.

CAPTAIN TOAD

SEEN IN:
Super Mario 3D World, Captain Toad: Treasure Tracker

SUPERPOWERS:
Pulling objects out of the ground

He can't jump, he can't run, and he's terrified of almost everything in his path. Has there ever been anyone less suited to heroic deeds than the cutesy Captain Toad? And yet he prevails in his quest for treasure, thanks to his determination. He pulls turnips out of the ground to throw at enemies and chips away at obstacles in his path using his trusted pickax. He might not have the same sort of superpowers you'll see elsewhere on these pages but that's the point—Captain Toad proves that sometimes, cuteness and determination can be pretty heroic.

PHOENIX WRIGHT

SEEN IN:
Phoenix Wright—Ace Attorney, Ultimate Marvel vs. Capcom 3

SUPERPOWERS:
Sharp observation, shouting "OBJECTION!"

"OBJECTION!" Phoenix Wright's trademark war-cry is accompanied by a dramatic point.

Phoenix Wright is always dressed in a suit, even when he's at the scene of the crime and looking for clues.

"OBJECTION!" Phoenix Wright fans will recognize his famous cry, as the attorney interrupts court proceedings. Phoenix Wright might seem like a fool, stumbling through investigations with no real clue, but his mind is always razor-sharp when it matters and the giant "OBJECTION!" speech bubble is a dramatic moment that puts everyone on edge. He can even use the speech bubble as an attack in *Ultimate Marvel vs. Capcom 3*.

THOMAS

SEEN IN:
Thomas Was Alone

SUPERPOWERS:
Big personality

We know what you're thinking—is that it? Thomas is just a red block? Well, that's definitely weird, but how can it be a super hero? Thomas qualifies as a super hero because for something without any expressions, limbs, or speech, he has a huge personality. As the story unfolds, you learn that he is an artificial intelligence trying to escape the computer mainframe he's been trapped in. The bravery of Thomas as he finds other AIs and leads them to safety puts most fuller-bodied super heroes to shame, while the humor and wit of this curious super hero will stay in your mind long after the credits roll.

> British comedian Danny Wallace narrates the story in *Thomas Was Alone*, as Thomas never speaks during the adventure.

> You don't just play as Thomas. You also play as other characters such as Claire and Chris, who, of course, are different colored blocks.

ROCKET RACCOON

SEEN IN:

Ultimate Marvel vs. Capcom 3

SUPERPOWERS:

Accomplished pilot, expert marksman

What Rocket Raccoon lacks in size, he makes up for with the stash of weapons he brings with him. Rocket Raccoon can use swinging logs, net traps, explosive mines, oil fires and sci-fi "Spitfire" pistols to harass his enemies, while his speed and size makes him a tough target to hit. Even better, if Rocket Raccoon does get into trouble, he can burrow underground and resurface when the danger passes. Rocket Raccoon proves that size doesn't matter. And also, neither does being a raccoon!

> Rocket Raccoon can use his "Rocket Skates" move to nip around in the air, which is useful if he needs to change direction in mid air.

> Rocket Raccoon's "Spitfire" move lets him fire two blobs of energy at his opponent, and he can aim each one individually.

RECREATING CIVIL WAR

The *Civil War* comic book storyline saw Iron Man and Captain America face off after a group of heroes accidentally hurt civilians with their powers. Iron Man felt partly responsible, and so worked with the US government to help put all heroes on a register, so that they could be called upon to help only when really needed. Captain America disagreed, arguing that if he saw someone in danger, he couldn't just stand by. The former friends had to fight for their own beliefs, and the result was an epic clash—on the page and the big-screen. Now you can relive the fight with these awesome games!

MARVEL PUZZLE QUEST

☆ Every player has to team up in this brilliant take on *Civil War*. You're up against Captain America or Iron Man but they have a massive pool of health, far higher than ordinary characters. This makes it impossible for one player to beat the leaders alone. Instead, everyone chips away at their health. Slowly but surely, with each member of your team doing damage, one of the leaders will fall. If you're on the winning side, then you unlock a five-star version of Iron Man or Captain America to use for yourself.

MARVEL CONTEST OF CHAMPIONS

☆ When you pick a side, you get different bonuses for all your fights. For example, side with Iron Man and your critical hits do more damage while Captain America allies are more likely to land critical hits. You can also help any other players on your side with their missions too, and they will come to your aid as well. You can also relive fights from the movie and comics, pitting Iron Man against Captain America, Captain America against Winter Soldier and so on.

MARVEL FUTURE FIGHT

☆ In this faction-vs.-faction battle, you earn points for your side by completing missions. The more points you earn, the more you push back against the rival side, with updates showing who's in the lead. After each day, the winning side is showered with rewards from ISO-8 crystals to power up characters to new heroes. As an added bonus, you can even unlock the uniforms worn in the *Civil War* movie!

MARVEL: PINBALL

Unlike the other games here, you don't pick your side before you play *Marvel: Pinball*. Instead, you pick your side *as* you play, deciding whether to team up with Iron Man or Captain America depending on where you hit the ball. Despite the game just being a simple pinball table, this still somehow captures the emotion and conflict at the heart of the *Civil War* movie. You have to choose a side, you have to gain allies, and then you have to go toe-to-toe with the leader of the rival faction. Who knew a pinball game could get so deep?

MARVEL HEROES

Marvel Heroes has had a wealth of updates for *Civil War* fans, too. The costumes from the movie were added to *Marvel Heroes*, along with missions that put you up against Crossbones. There are also daily missions that count towards building influence for your side. You can also take part in a *Civil War* tournament, with the winner being the team with the best performance. Best of all, if you play as a character involved with *Civil War* such as Vision or Scarlet Witch, you get bonus experience!

LEGO MARVEL'S AVENGERS

The free *Civil War* add-on can be downloaded by owners of LEGO *Marvel's Avengers* on PlayStation, and adds nine new characters from *Civil War* to the fray. These include Captain America, Iron Man (Mark 46), Agent 13, Black Panther, Crossbones, Falcon, Scarlet Witch, War Machine, and Winter Soldier. What about Spider-Man? The *Civil War* Spidey is available in a separate pack. Both packs are free!

MARVEL AVENGERS ACADEMY

Even a city-building game like *Marvel Avengers Academy* doesn't get left out of the *Civil War* fun! In the game, you have to complete different quests, depending on whether you side for or against mutant/super hero registration, with the story escalating until you face Hydra's biggest bosses. *Civil War* characters Winter Soldier and Black Panther have also been added to *Marvel Avengers Academy* as part of the *Civil War* celebration, so there is plenty of new stuff for you to enjoy.

MARVEL: ULTIMATE ALLIANCE 2

Marvel: Ultimate Alliance 2 doesn't just have a level or some characters from the *Civil War* storyline. The entire game is based on the famous plot from the comics, with branching storylines depending on who you side with. You even fight different bosses depending on your path—the likes of Cable, Hercules, and Dagger await if you side with pro-registration, while anti-registration players will battle Bullseye, Lady Deathstrike, and She-Hulk.

MIX+SMASH: MARVEL SUPER HERO MASHERS

The excitement of *Captain America: Civil War* brought one of its starring characters, Black Panther, to *Mix+Smash: Marvel Super Hero Mashers*. As *Mix+Smash* lets you build super heroes from different parts, you can add Black Panther's body parts to any super hero. Try Black Panther's head on Groot's body for a strangely unsettling combination.

STATS

20 **different** franchises including *Doctor Who* and *DC Heroes*

44 playable figurines

12 playable versions of The Doctor available

THE ULTIMATE DREAM TEAM

LEGO DIMENSIONS

DID YOU KNOW? Homer Simpson's dialogue is by his real voice actor, Dan Castellaneta... who also does the voice for Krusty The Clown!

⭐ **Once upon a time Batman, Gandalf, and Wyldstyle team up to battle the Wicked Witch of the West.** And then Homer Simpson, Scooby Doo, and Slimer help out. How completely bizarre, but totally awesome at the same time! And best of all, you get to create your own wacky scenarios. It's a combination of traditional LEGO gameplay seen in the likes of LEGO *Marvel Avengers* and toys-to-life figurines. You build the figurines and the portal yourself, while the gameplay changes depending on where you place the characters on the portal. What's more, there's no need for a sequel, as the developers keep on releasing new characters such as Sonic The Hedgehog and *Adventure Time*'s Jake and Finn for LEGO *Dimensions* instead. Every new pack helps you rewrite the rules all over again!

TIPS & TRICKS

⭐ **DON'T DO ALL THE ATTACKING**
You have other allies, controlled by the computer. Let them help attack enemies and do some of the work for you.

⭐ **SWITCH CHARACTERS**
When your character's health starts to run low, switch to another member of the team. Just remember that sooner or later, you'll need to get health back.

⭐ **SMASH IT UP**
If you're really struggling for health, smash the scenery around you to look for hidden hearts. It's not the most effective way to survive but it works!

TOP 5 BAD GUYS

STAY PUFT

1 You can grow large with Stay Puft and become the infamous city-stomping monster from the *Ghostbusters* movie. But you can also show off his cute side too. Stay Puft's naughty grin when he corners the Ghostbusters is replaced by a lovely smile, as he runs around with his arms stretched out wide with glee.

CYBERMAN

2 Even in the cute and colorful world of LEGO *Dimensions*, Doctor Who can't escape the Cybermen. At least you have a chance to play as the cyborgs this time round! It's lots of fun too, as Cyberman has cool tools to play around with including X-Ray Vision, Hacking, and Mind Control. Best of all, you can also ride around in a Dalek.

BAD COP

4 He might have a dual personality in *The LEGO Movie* but when it comes to LEGO *Dimensions*, Bad Cop always plays the part of . . . well, bad cop! Armed with a scorching-hot laser and deadly judo throw, Bad Cop has some brutal tools that let him deal out justice to those he deems to be breaking the law.

GOLLUM

3 His love for the One Ring led him and others to trouble in *Lord of the Rings*. In LEGO *Dimensions*, Gollum has somehow become even more trouble thanks to his fish, which he uses to slap enemies with! He also uses his fish as a boomerang. For an extra air of menace, Gollum also uses the hideous giant spider Shelob the Great to get around.

WICKED WITCH

5 Not only is Wicked Witch the first boss you face in LEGO *Dimensions* but she's also a playable character. Frustrated by her magic shields? Annoyed by her flying just out of reach so you can't hit her? You can do the same, using her magic spells to wreak havoc and clambering onto a flying monkey to get around.

SUPER SKILLS

With DC Comics, Doctor Who, Scooby Doo, Ghostbusters, The Simpsons, and more, LEGO *Dimensions* is crossover heaven.

BRAVERY	
MISCHIEF	
DESTRUCTION	
TEAMWORK	
FUN FACTOR	

★ MIX THEM UP
When you put a team together for Free Roam levels, pick characters with a wide variety of skills to try and cover as many of the puzzles as you can.

★ GET UP CLOSE
Don't be afraid to get close, even if low on health. It's much more effective to use melee attacks up close than it is to use projectiles from distance.

LEGO DIMENSIONS... DC COMICS HALL OF HEROES

ALL THE HEROES AND VILLIANS RATED!

BATMAN

☆VEHICLE
BATMOBILE

☆ABILITIES
GRAPPLE
BOOMERANG
STEALTH

POWER 9
ADAPTABILITY ... 8
TOUGHNESS 3
SPEED 3

AQUAMAN

0:24.75
0:08.19

POWER 6
ADAPTABILITY ... 9
TOUGHNESS 5
SPEED 7

☆VEHICLE
AQUA
WATERCRAFT

☆ABILITIES
DIVE
GROWTH
ATLANTIS
HAZARD
CLEANER

BANE

☆VEHICLE
DRILL DRIVER

☆ABILITIES
HAZARD PROTECTION
BIG TRANSFORM
SUPER STRENGTH

POWER 7
ADAPTABILITY ... 3
TOUGHNESS 10
SPEED 3

CYBORG

POWER 8
ADAPTABILITY ... 7
TOUGHNESS 9
SPEED 2

☆VEHICLE
CYBER-GUARD

☆ABILITIES
LASER
DIVE
SUPER STRENGTH
TARGET
BIG TRANSFORM
TECHNOLOGY

BANE'S DRILL DRIVER CAN BE UPGRADED TO BLOW UP SILVER BLOCKS!

HARLEY QUINN

POWER	7
ADAPTABILITY	2
TOUGHNESS	3
SPEED	8

☆ VEHICLE
QUINN-MOBILE

☆ ABILITIES
ACROBAT
SUPER STRENGTH

HARLEY'S SUPER STRENGTH COMES FROM THE GIANT HAMMER SHE CARRIES.

WONDER WOMAN

SUPERMAN

POWER	9
ADAPTABILITY	9
TOUGHNESS	10
SPEED	8

☆ VEHICLE
HOVER POD

☆ ABILITIES
FLYING
DIVE
INVULNERABILITY
LASER
DEFLECTOR
FREEZE BREATH
X-RAY VISION
SUPER STRENGTH

POWER	8
ADAPTABILITY	8
TOUGHNESS	7
SPEED	5

☆ VEHICLE
INVISIBLE JET

☆ ABILITIES
GRAPPLE
BOOMERANG
FLYING
DIVE
INVULNERABILITY
MIND CONTROL
DEFLECTION

THE JOKER

POWER	6
ADAPTABILITY	8
TOUGHNESS	4
SPEED	4

☆ VEHICLE
THE JOKER'S CHOPPER

☆ ABILITIES
GRAPPLE
TARGET
HAZARD
ELECTRICITY

WHO CAN STOP SUPERMAN?

INJUSTICE: GODS AMONG US

DID YOU KNOW?
The magician Zatanna, a fan favorite from DC's comics, was added to Injustice when fans voted for her in a Twitter poll.

☆ **Superman is one of the most powerful beings in the universe.** But what happens if he turns on us rather than helping us? That's the premise for *Injustice: Gods Among Us*, when Superman forms a regime that keeps the peace by any means necessary. As villains are drawn to his cause, heroes have to come together to stop Superman and make him realize the error of his ways. This one-vs-one fighting game draws in characters from the rich history of DC Comics, including lesser-known faces such as Killer Frost and Hawkgirl. Trying each character out is great fun because they all have brilliant special moves—The Joker uses chattering teeth as a weapon, Catwoman can whip her foes, and so on. And the mayhem begins all over again in *Injustice 2*, featuring Atrocitus, Supergirl, and Red Hood.

TIPS & TRICKS

★ **CLOSE OR FAR?**
You need to work out which range your character is best from. Cyborg and Sinestro work well at a distance while The Flash and Bane need to be up close.

★ **USE YOUR TRAIT**
Each character has a unique "trait." Aquaman can summon water to slip out of combos, for example. Use your character's trait as often as you can.

TOP 5 INJUSTICE CHARACTER TRAITS

BLACK ADAM'S LIGHTNING ORBS

1 Black Adam can summon three lightning orbs that constantly circle him, ready to zap anyone who dares step too close. Opponents can't just hide at a safe distance though, as Black Adam can also throw these lightning orbs at anyone trying to run away from him.

GREEN LANTERN'S POWER

2 For his trait, Green Lantern activates the power of his lantern ring. This temporarily powers up all his special moves, so they become more damaging and reach farther than before. Although the effect only lasts a few seconds, that might be all Green Lantern needs to win the fight.

HAWKGIRL'S FLIGHT

3 Hawkgirl gains the power of flight with her trait. She can hover freely for eight seconds, throwing maces from the sky where it's difficult for opponents to retaliate. Her flight works brilliantly as a defensive move too. If you're feeling pressured by your opponents' attacks, just fly out of harm's way and rethink your strategy.

ZOD'S WRAITH

4 Superman's nemesis summons a monster from the Phantom Zone that follows him around. This means Zod's foes now have to defend themselves from two threats, as Zod can carry on attacking while the monster swipes and bites from the ground. Zod can even take a step back from the fight, letting his summoned monster do all the work!

SINESTRO ORB

5 When Sinestro powers up his trait, he summons a tiny yellow orb that shoots a single shot of energy on his command. This single shot is small but can crack open the opponent's defense with ease. It will hit the opponent into the air and give Sinestro a chance to land big damage before they can recover.

SUPER SKILLS

It's Batman vs. Superman. Green Lantern vs. Sinestro. Harley Quinn vs. Wonder Woman. What more could you want?

BRAVERY
MISCHIEF
DESTRUCTION
TEAMWORK
FUN FACTOR

★ **SHOVE OPPONENT AWAY**
Press the "meter burn" button while blocking and this will push your attacker away. It will cost one bar of super meter but it's worth it just to get some space.

★ **DESPERATION SUPER**
If you're about to lose and you have a super attack ready to go . . . use it. Your opponent might be expecting this last-ditch tactic but it'll be your best shot to get back into the match.

BUILD THEM UP, BREAK THEM DOWN

MIX+SMASH: MARVEL SUPER HERO MASHERS

The title says it all. You mix up super heroes—putting Captain America's arms and Iron Man's head on Spider-Man's body, for example. Then you use your new mixed-up hero to smash your opponent's creation to pieces! *Mix+Smash* is so simple to play. You attack by tapping weak spots on your opponent, you defend by tapping the screen at the right time, and you can activate huge special moves. Powering up your special move is where skill comes into play—you either need to time your taps as icons appear on the screen, or draw a line through floating icons. Do this well and you'll literally smash the other player to bits!

DID YOU KNOW?

You can mix together parts from six different super heroes in *Mix+Smash*, creating your own super monster.

SUPER SKILLS

3
2
1

GROOT TAKES ROOT

HEAD BONUS
-25% DAMAGE

Literally smashing super heroes to pieces makes *Mix+Smash* one of the most delightfully destructive games ever made.

BRAVERY	
MISCHIEF	
DESTRUCTION	
TEAMWORK	
FUN FACTOR	

TIPS & TRICKS

★ CHECK YOUR BONUSES
Before a fight, check the bonuses awarded for building your hero a certain way. You might get a damage bonus for using Hulk's head, for example.

★ TAP THE SPOTS
To attack, just tap the spots as they appear on your opponent but do it quickly! Take too long and you'll miss the attack.

★ ACTIVATE SUPER
Always use your big super attack as soon as you unlock it, as this is the quickest way to finish off your opponent and win the match.

DID YOU KNOW?

The same publisher also published the brilliant WWE Immortals, where WWE superstars are re-imagined as super heroes!

ZOD VS. SUPERMAN

MAN OF STEEL

☆ **He's your mentor in *DC Universe Online*.** He's shrunk down to LEGO form in the LEGO *Batman* series. You can even use him to battle The Joker in *Injustice*. But rarely do you see Superman star in his own games. *Man of Steel* gives Superman the chance to shine, as he battles to save Earth from General Zod and his invading forces. From your sleepy hometown of Smallville to a dramatic final showdown in the Fortress of Solitude, Superman punches his way through Zod's army. The big moments come when you wear your foe down and wind up for a massive punch that hits them into cars, buildings . . . even up into the air. You can then fly after their spinning body and drag them into a new area to continue the fight!

SUPER SKILLS

In this dazzling showcase of his powers, Superman shows us exactly why he's one of the most iconic super heroes around.

BRAVERY	
MISCHIEF	
DESTRUCTION	
TEAMWORK	
FUN FACTOR	

TIPS & TRICKS

★**LEARN TO PARRY**
If you block at the last possible moment, you'll parry your opponent's blow, giving you a chance to strike back.

★**USE OBSTACLES**
During flying sections, drag your attacker through any obstacle you can. All obstacles do the same amount of damage.

★**BUILD UP HEAT VISION**
When you've connected enough attacks, you'll get to use heat vision. Upgrade this between fights because it's the best way to do quick damage.

BUILD YOUR OWN SUPER HERO TRAINING GROUND

MARVEL AVENGERS ACADEMY

⭐ We've seen Iron Man, Falcon, and the Hulk save the world many **times.** But who trained them to be the heroes you know and love? It turns out that you did! *Marvel Avengers Academy* places these super heroes under your tutelage, as you build a school where they can improve their powers, meet heroes, and undertake their first missions. Assign duties to each of your super-heroes-in-training— they become stronger and word of your academy soon spreads. As your number of students grow, you'll realize the trick is to make sure you devote enough time to each student while keeping troublesome students in line. This is definitely a game for those who can multitask.

DID YOU KNOW?

If Black Widow sounds familiar, that's because she's voiced by Alison Brie, the voice behind Unikitty in *The LEGO Movie.*

SUPER SKILLS

queenbee First day at Avengers Academy!! Got a new phone from @prettytony! Can't wait to hit a #hydra!!!!!! #firstday #wasprocks

Comment   Like

Whether they're practicing skills or getting to grips with social media, it's awesome to see our favorite heroes in training.

| BRAVERY |
| MISCHIEF |
| DESTRUCTION |
| TEAMWORK |
| FUN FACTOR |

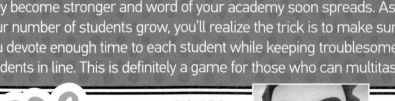

TIPS & TRICKS

★ **BUILD UP SHARDS**
Tasks take longer and longer to complete, so save some of the Shards you collect. These can be used to complete tasks instantly.

★ **TIME FOR COMBAT**
Some characters will complete fights quickly. Check which character will brawl fastest before sending them off to fight.

★ **BULLETIN BOARD**
Keep checking the bulletin board in the middle of the academy. If there are any exclamation marks, this means there's a new quest to do.

REAL AMERICAN HERO

CAPTAIN AMERICA: THE WINTER SOLDIER

CAPTAIN AMERICA: THE WINTER SOLDIER

DID YOU KNOW?
One of the first names considered for the character that would become Captain America was "Super American."

☆ There are few things more satisfying than throwing Captain America's shield and watching it ping around, taking out enemies. Except for maybe blowing up an abandoned car and seeing the explosion climb into the sky. Or perhaps calling Black Widow and watching her acrobatically eliminate her enemies. *Captain America: The Winter Soldier* piles on the action, as you clear out streets, investigate laboratories, and patrol rooftops. It's brilliantly paced as well, with small moments of downtime allowing you to catch your breath as the next group of guards slowly marches into view. For those who want endless bursts of action with explosive results, few games do it better than *The Winter Soldier.*

SUPER SKILLS 3224

x15
EXCELLENT!

With backup from S.H.I.E.L.D. agents and fellow Avengers, Captain America is a real handful for anyone in his way.

BRAVERY	
MISCHIEF	
DESTRUCTION	
TEAMWORK	
FUN FACTOR	

TIPS & TRICKS

★ USE YOUR SPECIAL ATTACK
Captain America has a special attack that takes a while to charge but is the most effective way of dealing with enemies. Use this whenever it is available.

★ ISO-8 UPGRADES
Use the Research tab between missions to build new ISO-8 crystals that will improve health, attack damage, and so on.

★ CALL UPON HELP
If you get really stuck, tap the Avengers icon in the corner to call for Black Widow's help, so she clears any threats ahead.

SUPER HERO COSPLAY

JENNIFER
@TRENDYNERDYCOOL

HARLEY QUINN
INJUSTICE 2

WHY COSPLAY AS HARLEY QUINN?
For me, Harley Quinn was one of those characters that has had so many different versions that I really enjoy the variety. With some characters, I'm not very enthusiastic about new versions, however, for a female character that didn't even technically begin in comics, the multitude of versions just shows how much everyone loves her.

WHY THE SUICIDE SQUAD VERSION?
I really like this version of Harley Quinn! Of course I appreciate the classic version, though I wasn't really crazy about the video game version, but this is a median between the two. The black and red catsuit and full face of makeup versus a much less modest version in the video games weren't really how I'd imagine Harleen. I think that the *Suicide Squad* version is not only modern, but also kind of edgy—in a cute way. It says "bad guy" in a way that is playful and dangerous at the same time without looking deranged, or scandalous.

WHAT'S YOUR FAVORITE SUPER HERO GAME?
I am a LEGO fanatic. I have played LEGO *Harry Potter*, *Batman*, *Star Wars*, and *Indiana Jones*. They are so much fun, but not as easy as they look! I've played others, but those remain my favorite.

BEN
@LYINGCATCOSPLAY

STAR-LORD
MARVEL FUTURE FIGHT

WHY DO A COSPLAY OF STAR-LORD?
I just love the character! Who wouldn't want to be a space pirate?

WHAT WAS THE HARDEST DETAIL TO GET RIGHT?
Without a doubt, the Walkman. After *Guardians* came out in the cinema, the price of Walkmans sky-rocketed!

WHAT SORT OF REACTION DID IT GET?
People loved it! We had an amazing day at LSCC (London Super Comic Con) and we were stopped for pictures every few minutes.

WHAT'S YOUR FAVORITE SUPER HERO GAME?
For me, it's got to be between *Injustice: Gods Among Us* and *Spider-Man 2*. *Injustice* perfectly captured the characters of the DC universe, and who doesn't love a good fighting game? *Spider-Man 2* is still the best super hero video game around. I plugged in my PS2 a couple of months ago, and the game still holds up.

WHAT'S YOUR DREAM SUPER HERO GAME?
A HD remake of *Spider-Man 2*!

LOCATION

Credit: Gallagher Photos

KAYLEY
@KAYLEYMARIECOSPLAY

WHY THOR?

Thor has always been one of my favorite characters; beyond the god of thunder's ferociousness is a character who doesn't just wake "being mighty," like most other super heroes. For Thor, there is a moment when the character has to wonder, "Am I worthy enough to carry Mjolnir today?" Thor has to earn

THOR
MARVEL FUTURE FIGHT

his (or her) worth. When I cosplay Thor, I feel powerful, strong. I see the hope and joy in adults and children alike. I become worthy.

WHAT WAS THE HARDEST PART OF THE COSTUMES TO GET RIGHT?

My current Thor cosplay was inspired by Jason Aaron's current run of *The Mighty Thor*, in which Thor is now a woman who is worthy enough to pick up Mjolnir, whereas the Odinson is no longer able to do so. When making any cosplay, there are especially challenging pieces. While I love making helmets, it is always difficult to find that perfect balance of weight and fit. You cannot have your helmet sliding around on your head, or being so heavy that you forgo wearing it at all due to discomfort; finding that balance is tricky. The cape attachment was another difficult creation— creating the drape and attaching it securely was not as easy as I thought it would be, especially because I chose a heavy fabric.

WHAT WOULD YOUR DREAM SUPER HERO VIDEO GAME BE?

Oh goodness, that is a tough choice. I am a huge fan of *The Legend of Zelda* series, I have played these games since I was very young. So I would have to say, if Marvel could create something with Thor, with a saga influenced by that genre, I think my video game soul would be very happy.

LUCY
@LYINGCATCOSPLAY

MYSTIQUE
LEGO MARVEL SUPER HEROES

WHY DO A COSPLAY OF MYSTIQUE?

I've always enjoyed the *X-Men* movies, with my favorite character by far being Mystique. I also enjoy the challenge of costume making, and Mystique's look is certainly quite a challenge! She's my perfect cosplay character.

HOW LONG DID IT TAKE TO PUT THE COSTUME TOGETHER?

I spent a total of 14 hours wearing the bodysuit while my husband Ben painted it with different types of fabric paints to achieve the scale effect. I couldn't have created or couldn't successfully wear this cosplay without Ben's help, he's a big part of the process. When I actually wear the bodysuit, it takes around two hours to complete the face, bodypaint, and hair.

WHAT WERE THE HARDEST DETAILS TO GET RIGHT?

The most difficult aspect is matching when I am cosplaying her, matching the color of the bodypaint of both the base color and the scales to the body suit. I still haven't been able to find a perfect match. It's frustrating because I'm a perfectionist!

WHAT SORT OF REACTION DID THE COSTUME GET?

When I wore her to LSCC 2016, she got a great reaction—lots of staring, photographs, compliments even from people who don't know the character well, and best of all, lots of questions and conversations with lovely people.

WHAT'S YOUR DREAM SUPER HERO GAME?

LEGO X-Men. Their own game!

STATS

More than **23** Marvel tables to play

Over 66,000 copies sold in its first month

8 tables based on the Marvel movie universe

Available on **9 platforms**

PINBALL WIZARD

MARVEL PINBALL

DID YOU KNOW?

The developers have also made pinball tables based on *Star Wars*, *Street Fighter II*, *Plants vs. Zombies*, and *South Park*.

☆ **Okay, this sounds simple.** It's Marvel and it's pinball, right? Wrong! This game takes pinball out of this world, adding comic book magic to each table. There are animated fights between heroes and villains, characters leap from bumper to bumper, and the ball even catches fire. There are also cool tricks like day turning to night as you play through the *Blade* table or the controls being inverted when you fight Mysterio on the *Spider-Man* table. There are 21 tables in total, from "*Fantastic Four*" to "*Guardians of the Galaxy*" to "*World War Hulk*." Each table has its own individual quirks to discover and secrets to unlock, as long as you have the dedication to find them. Best of all, you don't need to be a pinball fan to enjoy this—all Marvel fans are welcome.

TIPS & TRICKS

★ **EXAMINE THE TABLE**
Before playing, you can examine the table and zoom in on all the areas. This helps you learn where to go for high scores.

★ **GENTLE TO START**
When firing the ball, there's often an alternate route for higher points. Don't hit the ball with full power and see what happens.

TOP 5 TABLES

A-FORCE

1 In this table, focusing on some of Marvel's female heroes, the destruction of a Cosmic Cube has formed a Soviet-controlled alternate reality. You can control Black Widow and Madame Masque directly as they try their best to keep the Cosmic Cube balls alive in the table's Wizard Mode.

CHAMPIONS

2 Bombshell has robbed a bank on the Champions table, and it's up to Ms. Marvel, Squirrel Girl, and Spider-Gwen to stop her! You can use Squirrel Girl's Squirrel Army power to search for the enemy, and Spider-Gwen's webbing to trap him. It's one of the coolest levels ever.

ANT-MAN

3 This table follows the plot of the *Ant-Man* movie, in which Scott Lang, master thief turned super hero, takes on Yellowjacket. Shrink Scott down to the size of an insect, get multi-ball bonuses, and watch the hero fight it out on the table.

DOCTOR STRANGE

4 When evil forces from the dark dimensions attack the Earth, only one man can save the world— Doctor Strange. With his faithful servant Wong by his side and the help of loyal disciple Clea, the Master of the Mystic Arts faces multiple foes in an epic battle.

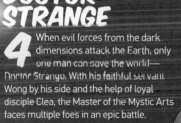

GUARDIANS OF THE GALAXY

5 This table starts with a bang, throwing out four balls as the Guardians escape the Kyln. From there, the action doesn't let up as Star-Lord, Gamora, Drax, Groot, and Rocket Raccoon fight off Yondu, Nebula, and even Ronan himself.

SUPER SKILLS

It's you versus a pinball table, while a host of Marvel heroes and villains crack their knuckles menacingly at each other.

BRAVERY
MISCHIEF
DESTRUCTION
TEAMWORK
FUN FACTOR

★ **BUMP THE TABLE**
If the ball looks like it's going to slip between flippers, bump the table. This nudges the ball aside and can save it at the last moment.

★ **LOOK FOR SECRETS**
Each table holds unique secrets that you can find by firing a ball into exactly the right place. Watch out for these shots and hit them for massive point scores!

MAKE YOUR OWN SUPER HERO!

POWER UP WITH THE INCREDIBLE SKYLANDERS IMAGINATORS

☆ If you've ever wanted to create your own super hero, with a unique collection of abilities and skills, then *Skylanders Imaginators* is the perfect game for you. In this game, you'll need to create your own customized character, which you can then use to battle the evil Lord Kaos. Once you've made your amazing hero, you can store them in a Creation Crystal, which will let you take your hero with you if you want to play the game at a friend's house.

You can assemble the body parts, then give your hero powers and abilities, before personalizing them with your favorite catchphrases. This really is the ultimate hero creation tool.

You might recognize one of the characters in the new game. Crash Bandicoot, who has his own series of games in the Nineties, now appears in *Imaginators*!

The plot of **Imaginators** is just as crazy as you might expect. Kaos has created a clone of himself to help take over the world. But the two Kaoses turn against each other, so you must team up with one to stop the other.

Every hero will be unique thanks to the cool creation tools. You can make your hero look as weird or as crazy as you like, and then add awesome special moves and clever catchphrases.

CAN WOLVERINE SAVE THE X-MEN?

UNCANNY X-MEN: DAYS OF FUTURE PAST

SUPER SKILLS

IT IS NEARLY MIDNIGHT, KATYA.

Time-traveling adventures await, as *Days of Future Past* follows Wolverine through an alternate timeline where most of the X-Men are imprisoned in Mutant Internment Camps. A fast-paced, side-scrolling beat-'em-up, you have to dance your way past enemy attacks and collect hidden XP canisters to unlock new moves for Wolverine. The main draw is the plot, with its dramatic twists and turns closely following the same storyline seen in the *Days of Future Past* comic. But all Marvel fans will find something to love here, as you'll get the chance to unlock old favorites like Storm and Colossus, while the enormous boss battles outdo most other games.

DID YOU KNOW?

The *Days of Future Past* storyline was first published in *The Uncanny X-Men* comic back in 1981.

The last few X-Men go up against Sentinel and Magneto. The results are explosive, as they try to save the world.

BRAVERY	
MISCHIEF	
DESTRUCTION	
TEAMWORK	
FUN FACTOR	

TIPS & TRICKS

★ PLAY AS SHADOWCAT
You start *Uncanny X-Men* playing as Wolverine but you quickly unlock Shadowcat. She's a much stronger character, so try her out.

★ UNLOCK LOCKHEED
Shadowcat's strongest skill is "Lockheed." This skill unlocks Lockheed, a dragon that attacks threats near Shadowcat.

★ 100 MEDALS
Keep an eye on your medal count. When it hits 100, you can unlock a new character like Colossus, Cyclops, Polaris, or Storm.

Ally Shifter

Lv.
★ ★
CALL ASSISTA

©+8

SERVING UP DESTRUCTION YOUR WAY ...

MARVEL FUTURE FIGHT

⭐ **Do you want to see the Hulk and Loki work together rather than against each other?** Maybe you want to see Spider-Man team up with Doctor Octopus? It's not just optional in *Future Fight*, it's almost encouraged. Adding variety to your squad of three means you can take out baddies with a wider range of special moves. Following up Iron Man's Hand Blasters with Ghost Rider's Motorcycle with M.O.D.O.K's Mind Attack isn't just effective, it's lots of fun too. As you do so you can watch as the screen lights up with spectacular colors and awesome special effects. Keep playing with your squad and they'll become stronger over time. Eventually, you can even take on other *Marvel Future Fight* squads online, in a battle to see which squad is the strongest.

SUPER SKILLS

Future Fight's explosive display of fireworks, sparks, and mayhem is high on both destruction and teamwork.

BRAVERY	
MISCHIEF	
DESTRUCTION	
TEAMWORK	
FUN FACTOR	

TIPS & TRICKS

★ KEEP ATTACKING
Future Fight doesn't have much in the way of defensive moves, and keeping your distance isn't effective, so it's best to keep attacking.

★ USE HEALERS
Some characters, like Groot, have moves that heal. This is the only defensive help you'll get so bring those characters for boss battles.

★ ATTACK EVERYONE
The best characters are those like Ghost Rider and Thor, whose attacks hit multiple targets rather than just one.

STATS

Over **75** heroes to unlock

5 Stars is the highest hero rating

6 Hero classes including Tech and Mystic

More than **14** stages to play on

28

THE ULTIMATE SHOWDOWN

MARVEL: CONTEST OF CHAMPIONS

DID YOU KNOW?
The debut movie for LEGO Ninjago is currently in the works and will hit the big screens in September 2017.

☆ **This is as pure as gaming gets.** You versus your opponent in one-on-one combat, with easy taps and swipes for attacks, rather than the complicated moves that you normally see in fighting games. The strategy seems simple at first, thanks to the rock, paper, scissors element to the attacks in *Contest of Champions*. Blocking stops light attacks, heavy attacks beat blocking, but light attacks beat heavy attacks. But that means you have to predict what your opponent will do next while staying unpredictable yourself. Add to that a wealth of special moves from Iron Man's Hand Blaster to Black Widow's acrobatic kicks and the end result is a frantic game that dares you to keep up.

TIPS & TRICKS

★ **LIGHT TO MEDIUM**
Soften up your opponent with light attacks and then switch to medium, for an easy, flowing combo that does good damage.

★ **PLAY TO YOUR STRENGTHS**
Each character has special traits, such as Hawkeye ability to drain his opponent's power. Use them!

★ **LEVEL UP**
If you're really struggling, remember you can play back through easier fights. This will level up your chosen fighter, so you come back stronger.

TOP 5 COOLEST HEROES

VENOM

1 Venom's special attacks are devastating, not only doing damage to his opponents, but also stealing some of their beneficial effects to give him a boost in battle. Add that to the improved stats Venom will gain if you pair him with any Spider-Man character or villain and you've got a really powerful fighter.

DOCTOR STRANGE

2 What makes Doctor Strange so devastating is that his power automatically increases as you fight. You don't need to land hits—his Special meter will charge up on its own—so you can unleash a really damaging attack. He also has some powerful passive abilities that make him an essential ally.

VISION

4 Android Vision is impervious to poisoning. His special attack uses his opponent's Power meter against them, doing more damage the more their meter is charged. Team him up with Iron Man, Ms. Marvel, or Scarlet Witch for extra Power stats, and a better chance of performing a Perfect Block.

WOLVERINE

3 Wolverine's Regeneration ability means that he regularly regains health—and this only increases as he takes more hits. If his bar is low, hold back to try and boost your health. As a Mutant champion, he's weak against Tech champions, but has an advantage over Skill champions, like Hawkeye.

SUPER SKILLS

SCARLET WITCH

16 HITS! ASTONISHING!

The ultimate game for one vs. one combat, these heroes put everything on the line in order to win.

| BRAVERY |
| MISCHIEF |
| DESTRUCTION |
| TEAMWORK |
| FUN FACTOR |

STAR-LORD

5 Add Star-Lord to a team with another Guardian of the Galaxy and you'll get a Synergy Bonus, which will either increase your armor or increase your chance of performing a Perfect Block. Plus, his Fury ability means his Attack power will increase every time he takes a hit.

★ **END WITH YOUR SPECIAL**
Use a special attack after you've connected with a medium attack, so your opponent can't block it.

★ **REMEMBER TO BLOCK**
Sometimes the best option is to wait for your opponent to attack and block. Then, strike back when he's vulnerable after your successful block.

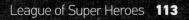

WHICH SUPER HERO ARE YOU?

WHAT'S YOUR IDEAL JOB?

A) Scientist
B) President
C) Wrestler
D) Actor

WHAT WOULD YOUR IDEAL SUPER POWER BE?

A) Exceptional intelligence
B) Telekinesis
C) Superhuman strength
D) Great one-liners

WHAT'S YOUR FAVORITE COLOR?

A) Gray
B) Green
C) Yellow
D) Red

WHERE WOULD YOUR SUPER HERO HEADQUARTERS BE LOCATED?

A) Hidden underground
B) Where evil can see and fear it
C) I don't need one
D) My house

WHAT SORT OF VIDEO GAMES DO YOU LIKE PLAYING?

A) Games that have just come out
B) Massively multiplayer online RPGs
C) Anything that is exceptionally difficult
D) Games I can play with my friends

WHAT ARE YOUR FAVORITE TYPE OF SUPER HERO MISSIONS?

A) Missions where I can show off my technology
B) The more important the mission, the better
C) Fighting against the odds
D) Anything fun with a big group of heroes

WHAT WOULD YOUR SUPER HERO SIDEKICK BE?

A) My best friend
B) All my friends
C) I'd rather work alone
D) Anyone as funny as me

WHAT WOULD YOUR SUPER HERO NAME BE?

A) Haxxor-01
B) Shield
C) Titan
D) Giggles

HOW WOULD YOU DESCRIBE YOUR HERO COSTUME?

A) Loaded with gadgets
B) Dominated by a large symbol
C) Dramatic with a cape
D) Bright and colorful

YOU ANSWERED MOSTLY ...

A GADGET FAN
Batman, Iron Man

Your mind is one of the greatest weapons you have. Why shoulder the heavy burden of being a super hero alone when technology can help you? You're just as happy creating gadgets as you are on the frontlines of the battle against evil.

B BORN LEADER
Professor Xavier, Green Lantern

Some people are just born to lead. They have the confidence and charisma to rally people to their cause. You might not realize it just yet but you are on the path to becoming a leader as well. People value your opinion on tricky matters before anyone else's.

C SYMBOL OF STRENGTH
Superman, Thor

Strong and defiant, you barely blink before charging into missions that others describe as impossible. Your inner strength matches your outer brawn. Your bravery means you're respected by your fellow heroes and feared by villains.

D FUN FRIEND
Star-Lord, Spider-Man

You always make light of a sticky situation, helping the group feel at ease. Loud and boisterous, you stand out as the center of attention but you're never selfish. You know that by drawing attention you're easing pressure on fellow heroes, and they love you for it.

HEROIC HALL OF DEEDS

Heroes are defined by their actions. Can you complete these gaming challenges and go from mortal to hero . . . or perhaps even legend?

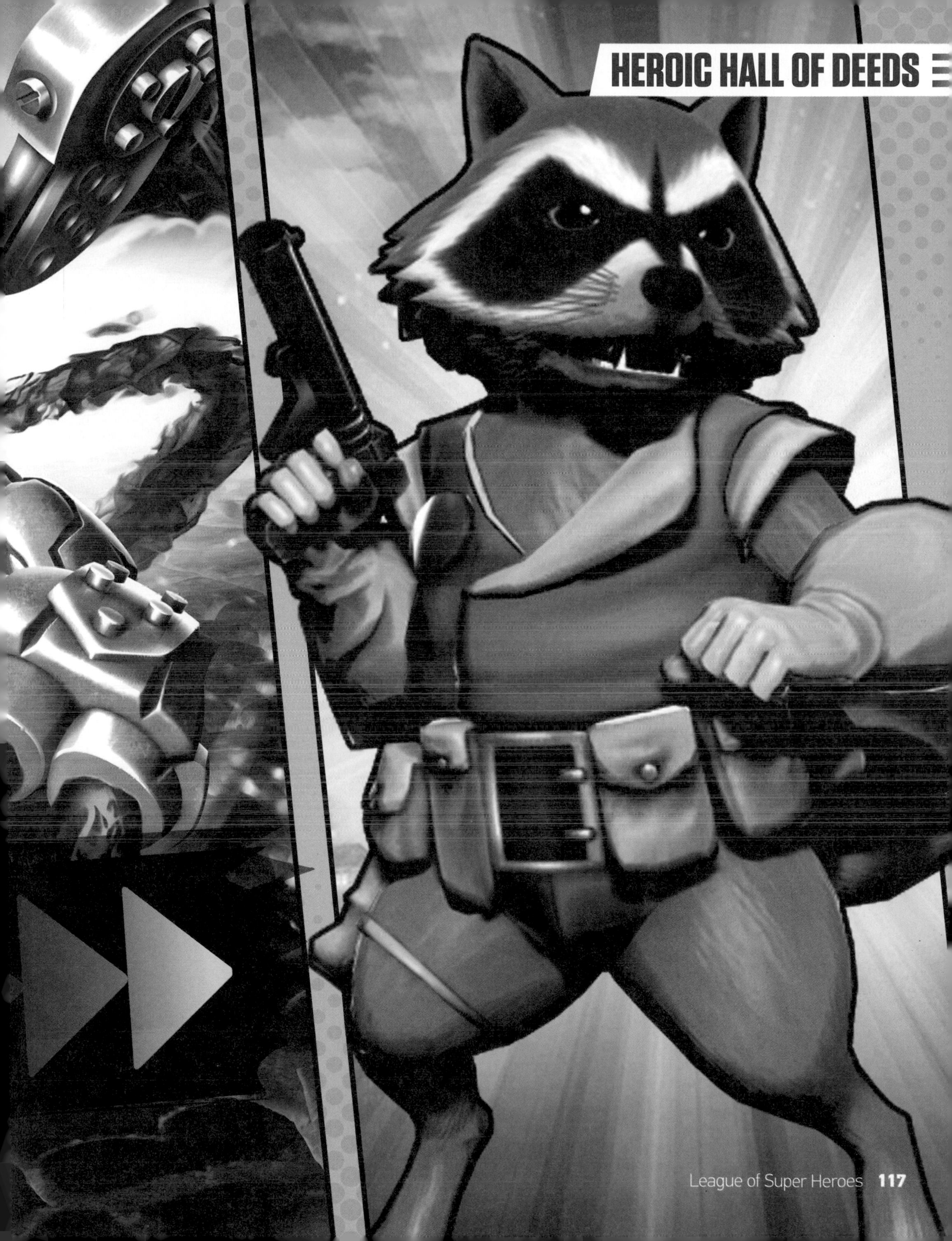

MORTAL FEATS

These are the daring deeds that even mere mortals can accomplish, on your way to joining the ranks of legendary super heroes.

9 HITS! AMAZING!

22

MARVEL CONTEST OF CHAMPIONS

Achieve a 20-hit combo

In most fighting games, "combos" are a string of attacks that your opponent doesn't even have a chance to block. However, *Marvel Contest Of Champions* keeps your combo counter going until you get hit or until you're forced to block. That means it's actually quite easy to clock up a 20-hit counter. First, you need to keep piling on the attacks and hope you get a little bit of luck with your opponent not striking back. If you do sense an enemy attack incoming, just retreat! Then when your opponent misses, you can dash back in and continue the combo. Make sure you don't have a character who's too powerful when you try this, as you might defeat your opponent before you get to 20 hits.

SKILLS TESTED

- ☆ TIMING
- ☆ PATIENCE
- ☆ STRATEGY
- ✔ TECHNIQUE
- ☆ SPEED
- ✔ DETERMINATION

Win with a character made of six different body parts

MIX+SMASH: MARVEL SUPER HERO MASHERS

☆ The idea behind *Mix+Smash* is you build your own super hero to march into battle. That means you can mix and match Spider-Man's head with Hulk's beefy arms, Captain America's chest, and Groot's spindly arms—and so on. Winning with body parts from different heroes isn't the tricky part of this challenge. It's unlocking all the body parts necessary to put your super hero together. You need to unlock six heroes to build a super hero where each body part is completely unique. You can scroll through unlocked heroes in the main menu, so keep track of how many you have unlocked and how many more you need.

SKILLS TESTED

☆ TIMING
☆ PATIENCE
☆ STRATEGY
☆ TECHNIQUE
☆ SPEED
✓ DETERMINATION

"FIND YOUR CHARACTER AND PLAY TO THEIR STRENGTHS"

Earn play of the game

PLAY OF THE GAME

OVERWATCH

☆ After each match of *Overwatch*, "Play of the Game" is shown. This is the standout moment from the game that's just taken place, as one player gets to bask in the spotlight for something special they did. The good news is that it's easier to qualify for this prestigious spot than you may think. All you need to do play to your character's strengths, which can be something as simple as reviving lots of your teammates with Mercy. So find your favorite character and use their skills effectively—whether it's protecting the team with Reinhardt, healing with Lucio, setting up turrets with Torbjorn, and so on. Just remember you'll need a bit of luck too, as you're competing with 11 other players!

SKILLS TESTED

☆ TIMING
☆ PATIENCE
☆ STRATEGY
✓ TECHNIQUE
✓ SPEED
✓ DETERMINATION

INCREDIBLE FEATS

You aren't a super hero just yet if you perform these deeds but you're well on your way to legendary status ...

Defeat one boss using just one character

MARVEL FUTURE FIGHT

Boss battles in *Marvel Future Fight* pit your team of three against one single opponent. This numbers advantage makes boss battles straightforward. Not only can you tag out any team members who have taken damage but you can also call upon the wider array of special moves your team has. So for a real challenge, try to beat the boss in a one-vs.-one scrap. You'll be surprised at how much tougher boss battles become when you can't tag out anymore, and it forces you to think tactically. Have I got the right character to for this fight? What moves do I need? If you manage to defeat any boss in a one-vs.-one battle, the experience will make you a much stronger *Marvel Future Fight* player.

SKILLS TESTED

- ✓ TIMING
- ☆ PATIENCE
- ✓ STRATEGY
- ✓ TECHNIQUE
- ☆ SPEED
- ✓ DETERMINATION

Otto Octavius, Doctor Octopus

HA!

RAPH
5924/10500

ASTRO ZOMBIE
3892/23000

703

TEENAGE MUTANT NINJA TURTLES: BATTLE MATCH

Connect 10 icons with a single move

You have to match icons to score points in *Battle Match*. Experience will see you grow from a player who tentatively matches three icons for low scores to a player who spots opportunities to set up longer matches of six or seven icons. For any serious *Battle Match* player, the real milestone is hitting double-digits and finally matching ten icons. The key is to set up the ten icon move by clearing out irrelevant icons first, so you clear the playing field and give yourself more room to maneuver. It seems tricky but mastering this technique is essential to climbing the high-score leaderboards. Eventually, what seemed impossible will become routine.

SKILLS TESTED

- ☆ TIMING
- ☆ PATIENCE
- ✓ STRATEGY
- ✓ TECHNIQUE
- ☆ SPEED
- ☆ DETERMINATION

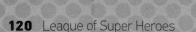

UNCANNY X-MEN: DAYS OF FUTURE PAST

Playing through *Uncanny X-Men* tests all sorts of gaming skills. You need to memorize the maps and where enemies appear. You need to the right strategy to defeat bosses. You need technique to pull off special moves. But to get through a level without dying demands a skill that isn't often required of super heroes—patience. You need to slowly pick your way through each level, making sure you don't take any needless risks. Remember when the health canisters are as well, just in case you do get hit.

Complete any level without dying

SKILLS TESTED

- TIMING
- ✓ PATIENCE
- ✓ STRATEGY
- ✓ TECHNIQUE
- SPEED
- DETERMINATION

HEROIC FEATS

These are the heroic deeds that call upon skill and technique not normally seen in mortal beings . . .

Unlock "Winner Takes All" Trophy

SKILLS TESTED

- TIMING
- ✓ PATIENCE
- STRATEGY
- ✓ TECHNIQUE
- SPEED
- ✓ DETERMINATION

DC UNIVERSE ONLINE

PlayStation owners will automatically receive a notification that they've unlocked this Trophy after they unlock every other Trophy in the game. Sound easy? There's a huge checklist of things to do, for every other trophy to unlock. You need to reach level 30 with three different characters, who use the Agile, Aerial and Swift move sets. You also need to reach level 30 with each of the mentors at least once. And you need to win a Platinum Medal, by posting an eye-wateringly quick time for any of the medal races dotted around Gotham and Metropolis. It's not that any of these tasks are *difficult* to do, but they will take you a long, long time to complete.

BATMAN: ARKHAM ORIGINS

⭐ The difficulty here isn't in beating Deathstroke, but ensuring you have enough health left to defeat him. You have to wipe out his army of foes first. Careless play against them means you'll be dragging a wounded, tired Batman into the final showdown against the one-eyed assassin. Just take your time. You don't need to choose defensive stance over assault stance to survive but you do need to attack slowly and carefully, so you can quickly block whenever you see a potentially devastating attack coming. Remember to switch to defensive stance to heal yourself if you do end up taking a lot of damage ...

SKILLS TESTED

- ✓ TIMING
- ✓ PATIENCE
- ✰ STRATEGY
- ✓ TECHNIQUE
- ✓ SPEED
- ✰ DETERMINATION

Defeat Deathstroke

THE EXPERT SAYS ...
STEPHEN ASHBY
Games Writer

I'm not ashamed to say that I was beaten plenty of times fighting Deathstroke in *Arkham Origins*. On the higher difficulty levels, your timing needs to be spot on every time to avoid his flurry of attacks, counter, and then start fighting back. It doesn't help that Deathstroke has a big metal stick and a katana, either—towards the end of the fight, taking a direct hit from his sword is devastating to your health.

But this isn't a criticism in any way. In the end, Batman isn't some super-human, with amazing abilities or laser-beam-shooting eyes. Like Deathstroke, he's just a guy. Swooping around over Gotham might make me feel like the Dark Knight, but nothing quite hammered home how vulnerable he could be than this boss battle.

Get three stars for every mission

THOR: THE DARK WORLD

⭐ There are a lot of missions to power through as Thor, as he fights the threat of Malekith and Loki. But what about the challenge of getting the maximum three stars for every mission? Each mission has different criteria that need to be met for each star to be unlocked—it could be that you have to complete the mission in a fast time, ensure your base doesn't take too much damage, survive without summoning Einherjar to fight by your side and so on. Save your coins for the Golden Armor and upgraded Einherjar for missions where you can take them—particularly Lancer and Valkyrie—as this will ensure you have the versatility and strength to blitz those missions to gain maximum star ratings.

SKILLS TESTED

- ✰ TIMING
- ✰ PATIENCE
- ✓ STRATEGY
- ✓ TECHNIQUE
- ✓ SPEED
- ✓ DETERMINATION

"YOU DO NEED TO ATTACK SLOWLY AND CAREFULLY"

SUPER HEROIC FEATS

These are the amazing achievements that push your skills to the limit and prove you have earned super hero status.

SKYLANDERS SUPERCHARGERS

The nefarious Skylanders villain is the last foe you face at the end of *Skylanders SuperChargers*, and this is the toughest Kaos has ever been in any game. The Emperor has a wide range of attacks that he harasses you with, such as spiked wheels that roll toward you, floating swords, waves along the cubed floor, and multiple versions of himself. As the fight reaches its dramatic climax, you have to deal with all of these attacks at the same time, and the sudden spike in difficulty might make you sweat under pressure! It takes patience and timing to weave your way around Kaos' attacks and land attacks of your own. A true test of any gamer.

Defeat Emperor Kaos

SKILLS TESTED

- ✓ TIMING
- ✓ PATIENCE
- ✓ STRATEGY
- ✓ TECHNIQUE
- ✓ SPEED
- ✓ DETERMINATION

Defeat General Zod on Kent's farm without upgrading

SKILLS TESTED

- ✓ TIMING
- ✓ PATIENCE
- ✓ STRATEGY
- ✓ TECHNIQUE
- ✓ SPEED
- ✓ DETERMINATION

MAN OF STEEL

Despite being very early on in *Man of Steel*—this showdown takes place in chapter four of the game's 18 chapters—this is a dramatic and sudden difficulty spike. General Zod comes with four blocks of armor rather than the standard two and is far more aggressive than the previous enemies you've faced. For an extra challenge, try not to upgrade Superman until you defeat General Zod. You won't have Heat Vision and you'll have to play defensively, parrying Zod's attacks as they come in. But survive this fight and your dodging and parrying skills will serve you well for the rest of the game.

Defeat all S.T.A.R. Labs with three stars

INJUSTICE: GODS AMONG US

★ S.T.A.R. Labs mode is what sorts the weaker *Injustice* players from the heroic ones. Over the course of its 240 missions, your skills will be stretched in a variety of unusual ways. You'll have to fight Cyborg while avoiding falling debris, dodge past chattering teeth and pies to apprehend The Joker, break into a safe in Wayne Manor, race Superman around the globe, bat away Sinestro's constructs and more. You need three stars for every mission, which means completing S.T.A.R. Labs isn't good enough—you need to thoroughly ace it!

SKILLS TESTED

- TIMING
- ✓ PATIENCE
- ✓ STRATEGY
- ✓ TECHNIQUE
- ✓ SPEED
- ✓ DETERMINATION

LEGENDARY FEATS

Only the most legendary super heroes can accomplish these deeds . . . are you one of the rare few?

On the Captain America table, defeat Red Skull

MARVEL PINBALL

★ This isn't just the trickiest task on the Captain America table, but the single trickiest task for any of the *Marvel Pinball* tables. You have to defeat Red Skull in a brawl but the only way to do that is to hit the ramps to either side of the Cosmic Cube or the Red Skull ramp right next to it. You can't hit any other ramps, which means you need perfect aim and you also need to remain calm under pressure. All it takes to ruin this heroic deed is one panicked shot to go astray. Hit the Cosmic Cube ramps or the Red Skull ramps five times and Captain America will beat down his nemesis at the top of the table.

SKILLS TESTED

- ✓ TIMING
- ✓ PATIENCE
- ✓ STRATEGY
- ✓ TECHNIQUE
- ✓ SPEED
- ✓ DETERMINATION

✓ Find and defeat Chef Pepperjack

SKYLANDERS TRAP TEAM

Defeat Chef Pepper Jack on Nightmare difficulty

SKILLS TESTED

- ✓ TIMING
- ★ PATIENCE
- ✓ STRATEGY
- ✓ TECHNIQUE
- ✓ SPEED
- ✓ DETERMINATION

If you thought you were good at *Skylanders*, think again. Chef Pepper Jack is a tricky villain to defeat on standard difficulty but tackle him on Nightmare and it becomes the hardest boss battle ever! His explosive peppers coat almost the entire arena in scorching hot lava. You have just a sliver of room to move around, which makes his charge attacks even harder to dodge. He fires up dense laser grids, which change pattern at a moment's notice and catch you out if you don't have razor-sharp reactions. Worst of all, on Nightmare difficulty, Chef Pepper Jack soaks up a ludicrous amount of damage, which means you have no margin for error.

"IT BECOMES THE HARDEST BOSS BATTLE EVER"

Defeat Daken

SKILLS TESTED

- ★ TIMING
- ✓ PATIENCE
- ✓ STRATEGY
- ✓ TECHNIQUE
- ✓ SPEED
- ✓ DETERMINATION

MARVEL PUZZLE QUEST

As part of the Juggernaut chapter in *Marvel Puzzle Quest*, you can choose the challenges running along the bottom of the mission screen rather than the top. The challenges along the bottom lead to a battle against Wolverine's son, the Dark Avengers variant of Daken. He heals three percent of his health every turn, unless there are less than nine blue tiles, then he *loses* three percent. Whenever anyone makes a green match on the board, Daken adds a red strike tile, which does five times more damage. He's also backed up by two analysts. You have to target blue tiles to shut down his healing effect and red tiles, to neutralize the threat of red strike tiles ... all while building your own super attacks and stopping Daken from landing big tile combos! Finding the right balance is tricky but if you're struggling, revisit earlier missions and grab some of the rewards they offer—unlocked comic books, for example, will help you level up your team.

SUPER HERO GAME GLOSSARY

AMIIBO
A small character figurine made by Nintendo that adds special functionality when held up to a sensor on the Wii U or 3DS in an amiibo-compatible game.

ASSIST
Some super hero games let you call in allies to temporarily jump into the battle, perform attacks, then leave again. This is known as an "assist."

CAMEO
The term used to describe a special person or character who makes a brief, surprise appearance in a movie or game. For example, Stan Lee, creator of many of Marvel's most famous heroes, often appears in Marvel movies and games for just a few seconds.

CIVIL WAR
One of the most famous storylines in comics. *Civil War* saw Marvel's comic book heroes fight each other over the idea of super heroes "registering" with the government, so they have accountability for their actions.

COOLDOWN
To keep players from using special attacks over and over again, most of them have a "cooldown." This means that after you use the attack, you have to wait a certain amount of time before you can use it again.

CO-OP
Short for co-operative, this is when you play with your friends (online or locally), rather than playing against them competitvely.

DOWNLOADABLE CONTENT (DLC)
This is extra content, such as levels or characters, that can be downloaded after a game has been released.

ENDLESS RUNNER
A popular mobile gaming genre in which your character will automatically move, and you have to jump or duck over the obstacles in the way. These games usually keep going until you hit an obstacle.

F2P
Free-to-play. These games are free downloads, so you don't have to pay anything to play them.

FREE ROAM
In LEGO games, completing levels will unlock them for Free Roam or Free Play modes. These modes will let you replay the level using any characters that you want to try.

HEALTH
Characters in super hero games usually have a health bar, which goes down every time they are hit by an attack. Health is usually represented by numbers (*Marvel Future Fight*), hearts (the LEGO games) or a bar (*Injustice: Gods Among Us*).

ISO-8 CRYSTALS
These are in-game crystals that give you the ability to boost your hero's skills, seen in games such as *Marvel Puzzle Quest* and *Marvel Contest of Champions*.

MELEE

Close-up attacks with fists or a short-range weapon are called "melee attacks." Characters such as The Hulk, are often called "melee characters."

MENTOR

Someone who trains you in the ways of becoming a super hero or villain. *DC Universe Online* allows you to choose a mentor, such as Batman or Lex Luthor.

MJOLNIR

The famous hammer wielded by Thor. It can only be used by someone "worthy" of wielding it, and holds immense power thanks to the magical enchantments cast upon it.

MMO

Massively Multiplayer Online. These games put players in a huge online world, along with all the other people playing.

MMORPG

An MMO with role-playing game elements. This usually involves creating your own character, and then fighting other players or enemies in the game world to make your character stronger, with new gear, skills, and weapons.

OVERHEAD ACTION GAME

A game which uses an overhead camera angle to give you a top-down view of the action.

PLATFORMER

A game in which you guide your hero through levels that involve tough jumps, enemies to defeat, and items to collect. 2-D platformers usually see the character running from left to right.

SPECIAL MOVE

Super heroes (and villains!) have "special moves" which are bigger, more effective ways of dealing with enemies. Ghost Rider can summon his flaming motorcycle to clear a path for him, for example.

SUPER MOVE

A one-off attack that's even more spectacular and damaging to the opponent. These attacks usually involve an expensive cost. For example, in *Injustice: Gods Among Us*, you have to build up a meter to use your Super Move.

Contents

Emerald tree boa

The rainforests of South America are home to the emerald tree boa. Its green colouring makes it hard to see amongst the trees. This helps it to make surprise attacks on its prey.

This snake spends a lot of its time off the ground. It grips the branches with its long, strong tail.

Baby boas

When they are born, emerald tree boas are yellow, orange or red. They change to bright green after about one year.

Special parts on the snake's head can sense heat given off by other animals. This helps the snake to find its prey.

The white markings on the snake's body break up its outline to make it harder to see.

5

Leaf-cutter ants

Central American leaf-cutter ants bite off pieces of leaves and carry them to their nest. There, they chew the leaves into a pile of mush, which rots and grows a type of fungus that the ants like to eat.

Ants live in a colony, which is a big group of about five to eight million ants.

Mandibles are sharp mouthparts that the ants use for cutting out and carrying pieces of leaves.

The ants need to collect the right kind of leaves to make their food. The leaves are found on the forest floor, or high up in the trees.

Plant food

Like the ants' fungus, you can add rotted raw vegetables to your garden soil to help the plants grow.

Leaf-cutter ants are able to carry leaf pieces more than 20 times their own body weight!

Three-toed sloth

This unusual creature is the world's slowest-moving animal. It hangs upside down in the rainforest trees and hardly ever comes down to the ground. It can eat, sleep and raise its young while hanging safely in the branches.

In the rainy season, a sloth's long fur gets covered with tiny green plants that help to hide it from predators.

Baby sloths cling onto their mothers using their claws, and stay with them until they are six months old.

A sloth will stay completely still if it senses a predator close by.

Sloth or bear?
Sloth bears were named by scientists who wrongly believed they were part of the sloth family.

In the treetops

Many rainforest animals can be found high up in the trees. The jaguar is a type of big cat. It is a good climber and may lie on a branch to rest or wait for prey. Harpy eagles are hunting birds that swoop through the forest in search of food.

The harpy eagle is one of the rainforest's most feared predators. It hunts sloths, snakes, lizards and macaws.

Fast movers

A spider monkey can move quickly between branches in the rainforest by using its hands, feet or tail.

The rainforest is home to thousands of types of plants and trees. The tallest trees can be up to 80 metres high!

Jaguars rest during the day and hunt at night. They like to eat peccaries – animals that look similar to pigs.

The blue morpho butterfly is one of the largest butterflies in the world.

Crimson topaz hummingbird

This beautiful bird lives in the middle and top levels of the rainforest. It feeds on nectar, a sugary liquid made by flowers. Hummingbirds can hover in mid-air like helicopters as they poke their long beaks into flowers to feed.

Most hummingbirds catch insects to feed to their chicks. This kind of food helps the chicks to grow quickly.

Bird nest

Female hummingbirds make nests from leaves and feathers. After they lay their eggs, they sit on them to keep them warm to help them to hatch.

Hummingbirds are named for the humming noise made by their flapping wings. The noise becomes louder as their wings beat faster!

This brightly coloured hummingbird is a male. Females are green and have short tails.

Hovering and flying use so much energy that a hummingbird has to feed about four times each hour.

Tree kangaroo

Slow and clumsy on the ground, tree kangaroos spend most of their time in trees. They feed on leaves, fruit and mosses, and sometimes even young birds. Tree kangaroos are related to common kangaroos and wallabies.

Carry me!

All types of kangaroo have a pouch in which their babies are carried.

A long tail helps the tree kangaroo to balance.

A tree kangaroo's ears are furry inside. This helps to keep out creepy-crawlies such as ticks or leeches.

Strong, curved claws help the tree kangaroo to grip branches as it moves through trees.

15

Red-eyed tree frogs

These bright-eyed frogs are small enough to fit in the palm of your hand. They live in the Central American rainforests. Frogs eat bugs such as moths, beetles, flies and crickets, and some may even eat smaller frogs!

A tree frog hides from predators by closing its eyes, tucking its feet underneath its body, and staying very still.

This frog has big eyes to watch out for hungry predators such as snakes, birds, bats and lizards.

Colour code
Some frogs are brightly coloured to warn that they are poisonous. Can you think of any other poisonous animals?

Special sticky pads on their toes help tree frogs to grip branches and flowers as they climb.

Bengal tiger

There are five types of tiger living around the world. All of them are endangered, so there aren't many of them left in the wild. This mother tiger is prowling through the forest with her cubs.

Striped fur helps tigers to blend in with the tall grass at the edge of the rainforest.

Cute cubs

Sometimes, tigers are born with white fur instead of orange. White cubs are often bigger than their orange brothers and sisters.

Tiger cubs stay with their mother until they are about two years old. She teaches them how to hunt.

A tiger's good eyesight helps it to hunt at night. It uses its sensitive whiskers to feel its way around.

Tigers are big and heavy so they don't run after their prey. Instead, they silently follow it, and then pounce!

Toco toucan

This strange-looking bird lives high up in the trees. It is the largest of all the types of toucan. Although its beak is enormous, it is very light, so the bird can still fly.

The brightly coloured beak helps the toucan to attract a mate.

The beak has a jagged edge to help the toucan bite fruit. The bird flicks its head backwards to drop the food into its throat.

20

Good eyesight helps the toucan to spot predators such as jaguars and birds of prey.

Beak shapes

A macaw is a type of parrot that lives in the same rainforest as the toucan. Its beak is a different shape to help it crack open nuts to eat.

In the water

Many animals in the rainforest stay close to rivers and pools. It is important for them to have water to drink. Tapirs and capybaras are good swimmers and can escape from predators by diving underwater.

Capybaras look like giant guinea pigs. They spend a lot of time in water and have webbed toes to help them to swim.

Downpour

Heavy rain all year means the rainforest is lush and green, and rivers are always full.

Tapirs often feed on plants along riverbeds, but they must be careful to avoid crocodiles.

Green iguanas swim using powerful strokes from their long tail.

Fun facts

Emerald tree boa Boas catch small birds and mammals by hanging tightly to a branch and grabbing their prey with their sharp teeth.

Leaf-cutter ants These ants are sometimes called 'parasol ants' because they carry leaves over their heads like a parasol, which is a kind of umbrella.

Three-toed sloth A sloth may sometimes lick the tiny green plants from its fur for a quick, tasty snack.

Jaguar A jaguar cub learns to hunt by living with its mother for at least two years.

Harpy eagle Female eagles lay two eggs, but once the first egg has hatched, the other is ignored and doesn't hatch.

Crimson topaz hummingbird These small birds carry pollen from flower to flower while they feed. This helps plants to spread through the rainforest.

Tree kangaroo Most of their time is spent in trees, but when tree kangaroos do come down to ground level they walk instead of hop.

Red-eyed tree frogs When a tree frog eats, it has to blink. The blinking action helps it to swallow food.

Bengal tiger A tiger doesn't always eat all of its prey in one go. It sometimes covers the animal with leaves and comes back to eat more later.

Toco toucan Its long, pointed beak helps the toucan to reach fruit on thin branches that would break if the bird perched on them.